GROUP COUNSELING

A PREFACE TO ITS USE
IN CORRECTIONAL AND WELFARE AGENCIES

BY

NORMAN FENTON, Ph.D.

GREENWOOD PRESS, PUBLISHERS
WESTPORT, CONNECTICUT

Library of Congress Cataloging in Publication Data

Fenton, Norman, 1895-
    Group counseling, a preface to its use in correct-
tional and welfare agencies.

    "Originally published ... by the County Project in
Correctional Methods, Sacramento, California, under the
auspices of the Institute for the Study of Crime and
Delinquency."
    1. Group counseling. 2. Corrections. 3. Public
welfare.
    [HV9275.F4 1974]   365'.66   73-9254
    ISBN 0-8371-6997-6

This Publication has been made possible
by a grant from

THE ROSENBERG FOUNDATION
of San Francisco, California

Originally published in 1961 by The County Project in
Correctional Methods, Sacramento, California, under the
Auspices of the Institute for the Study of Crime and
Delinquency

Reprinted with the permission of American Justice Institute

Reprinted in 1974 by Greenwood Press, Inc.,
51 Riverside Avenue, Westport, CT 06880

Library of Congress catalog card number 73-9254
ISBN 0-8371-6997-6

Printed in the United States of America

10 9 8 7 6 5 4 3 2

TO ALL MY FELLOW WORKERS

WHOSE FAITHFUL EFFORTS AND LOYAL COOPERATION

MADE POSSIBLE THE DEVELOPMENT

OF GROUP COUNSELING

IN THE PRISONS OF CALIFORNIA

FOREWORD

Group counseling, as described in this volume, has been used in the state prisons and honor camps of California since 1954. It has also been conducted at various times in county jails and rehabilitation centers, and continuously for a number of years in the honor camps of San Diego County. Pilot studies have also indicated possibilities for the use of somewhat similar group procedures with clients on public assistance in county welfare departments.

This book, prepared for those participating in the County Project in Correctional Methods, has drawn upon Part I of a volume used by prison employees.* Those who plan to use group counseling in their work should also read Parts II and III of this earlier text; copies of which have been given to the cooperating county agencies. Undoubtedly, there is a core of similarity in the conduct of group counseling with all kinds of subjects and in all types of agencies. However, when employed with clients in welfare departments or with youthful institutional inmates or probationers, it may be found that the methods used may need to differ somewhat from those found to be effective with men and women in prison.

The County Project in Correctional Methods is under the auspices of the Institute for the Study of Crime and Delinquency of Sacramento. It was made possible by a grant from the Rosenberg Foundation of San Francisco. A State Advisory Committee and local Sponsoring Committees have also been helpful in its development.

---

*   Fenton, N., "An Introduction to Group Counseling in Correctional Service", with a Foreword by Richard A. McGee. Revised edition, New York, The American Correctional Association, 1957, 204 pp.

Through the interest of Director Richard A. McGee of the Department of Corrections, Robert M. Harrison, Departmental Supervisor of Group Counseling, has served as an advisor to the Project. In addition to other assistance, Mr. Harrison read the text of this book critically and made a number of suggestions which have improved its meaningfulness.

Director J.M. Wedemeyer and Arthur W. Potts of the Department of Social Welfare, assigned Richart T. Van Metre, Jr., a Public Assistance Specialist, to collaborate in this Project. He has made many helpful suggestions regarding the program. Mr. Van Metre contributed thoughtful editorial suggestions regarding this manuscript which have increased its value especially for workers in welfare agencies.

My wife, Jessie Chase Fenton, read the manuscript critically. Her editorial suggestions have greatly enhanced its interest and clarity.

Mrs. Marianne Thomas, secretary of the Project, was of great assistance in the preparation of the copy for the printer. Her typing of the final manuscript and careful proof reading were important contributions to the book.

NORMAN FENTON

Carmel, California
February 20th, 1961.

CONTENTS

CHAPTER 1

INFLUENCES WITHIN A GROUP

HOW PEOPLE ARE AFFECTED IN A GROUP:

In ordinary life, as the reader is well aware, the presence of a given group seems to have special effects upon the attitudes and behavior of people. An adolescent at home with his parents may behave quite differently from the way he comports himself when with a group of his· peers or even with other adults.

Another means of recognizing the psychological interaction of people is to think of the effects upon you of the presence of other members of the congregation at a religious service. Emotional experiences at such times may be colored by the presence of the group. The feeling-tones may be heightened and frequently result in a deeper and somewhat different emotional experience than that which one feels in solitary worship.

Obviously, a more complicated analytical approach to an understanding of the psychological influences affecting individuals in a group could be obtained by relating them to the larger social group or the culture in which they grew up. Thus, a person's religious attitudes are affected by the religious culture to which he has been subjected in the impressionable years of childhood and adolescence. The effect of a group religious experience upon culturally different persons, thus, would vary with their backgrounds. The reader may find a wealth of interesting material in the writings of social anthropologists dealing with the influences of cultural factors upon human personality.

In their comprehensive study of the dynamics

7

of group life*, Wilson and Ryland have ably summarized the psychological influences of the group upon
personality in the following quotation:

> "Human beings can be understood only in re-
> lation to other human beings. What a man is,
> is reflected by the behavior of other men to-
> ward him. What a man thinks of himself is his
> judgment of the reactions of other men to him.
> The behavior pattern of any individual is a
> mirror of his total life-experience, most of
> which is in groups. If one is to understand an
> individual, one must know the groups to which
> he belongs. Every individual has a different
> status in each of the variety of groups to
> which he belongs. The same individual will ex-
> hibit different patterns of behavior in dif-
> ferent groups."

Two awesome examples of group interaction are
the behavior of people in a panic or during a riot.
At such times, people seem to be catapulted into ex-
tremities of fearful or aggressive action, often
quite different from their ordinary behavior. In
more commendable contrast, we may observe in times
of disaster or other periods of extreme danger that
individuals may display unusual qualities of heroism
and altruism, which are probably called out, at least
in part, by the effects of group interaction.

CONSTRUCTIVE EFFECTS OF GROUP INTERACTION:

Most people can profit from planned experiences
in constructive group interaction. For example, its
effects for improving morale have been strikingly
demonstrated in military agencies. One article de-

---

* Wilson, G., and Ryland, G., "Social Group Work
Practice," Boston, Mass., Houghton Mifflin Co.,
1949, page 37.

scribes group meetings in the naval units, which the originators have called "intensive bull sessions."* To quote from the article, "Several times each week, whenever units can be gathered for even 20 minutes, officers and petty officers are learning that their men are hungry for the American idea. I saw young imaginations begin to glow and then come afire in these sessions, as men began fully to understand, incredibly, for the first time in their lives, the American theory of the dignity and worth of the individual as expressed in the Declaration of Independence and the Constitution." The article goes on to recount the constructive effects of such group interaction in the form of better attitudes toward the service (more re-enlistments), better behavior, (fewer disciplinary offenses), and in other evidences of improved morale of the naval units involved.

Group interaction has also been used advantageously in influencing the attitudes and behavior of those cared for in health, welfare, or correctional agencies. An example is the group discussion program for expectant mothers conducted by nurses under the auspices of the American Red Cross and in collaboration with various health agencies. The women who go to pre-natal clinics not only receive individual attention, but are also encouraged to attend discussion groups where they may ask questions or express their feelings in regard to their problems. Under good leadership, they not only seek concrete explanations and directions in regard to their health and physical care during pregnancy, but those present also tell how they feel about many matters of general concern to them. For example, certain aspects of their relationships with the members of their families may be discussed. In talking about

---

*   Hubbell, J.G., "The Reader's Digest", 1960, May, pages 37-42. Abstracted from an article in the Navy Blue Book.

intimate personal matters they may reveal areas of deep sensitivity. These include how they are affected by their change in appearance or the way they react when morbidly curious people stare at them. Prospective mothers who have attended these sessions report that they have gotten considerable psychological help from the group. Talking about their situation frankly with other pregnant women and realizing that their own anxieties are not unique or exceptional seems to have a wholesome effect upon the morale of these expectant mothers.

Physiotherapists have for many years been aware of the values of groups. Remedial exercises engaged in by a group by persons with physical handicaps are regarded as more effective because of the psychological interactions therein than are the identical exercises when undertaken by patients when alone. The same factors of mutual acceptance, encouragement, and helpfulness are present as noted in the groups for prospective mothers.

THE ALCOHOLICS ANONYMOUS PROGRAM:

One of the good examples of constructive group interaction may be observed in the Alcoholics Anonymous program. This is a group treatment device, conducted by laymen, of which many psychologists and psychiatrists speak with appreciation. It has been accepted as one of the best examples of how people help each other in groups. The Alcoholics Anonymous program is not a "cure" for alcoholism, but rather a means of enabling the alcoholic to control his defect by means of constructive group interaction. The concepts and methods underlying the program of Alcoholics Anonymous have spread to other areas of social maladjustment. There are groups banded together to support each other in combatting the use of narcotics and the costly urge to gamble excessively and disastrously.

The person who is blind, the amputee, and others

with serious problems of social adjustment may, likewise, be assisted to live more comfortably with their handicaps by group methods resembling in some ways those of Alcoholics Anonymous. The group leader is able to guide the group, and the group members to assist one another, in focussing upon their strengths or potential strengths rather than being overwhelmed by their limitations and weaknesses. As in Alcoholics Anonymous, the feelings of belonging to the group and finding acceptance and support therein are not curing the handicap but, by alleviating the life situation somewhat, can make a wholesome adjustment more likely. Gisela Konopka has emphasized the importance of the phenomenon of acceptance in groups in stating that "the pattern of a group grows out of the forces of acceptance and rejection."*

The feelings of belonging are brought out in the Alcoholics Anonymous groups by the genuine and friendly interest in each other of those present at the meetings. Few, if any, groups in the community accept parolees more sincerely and genuinely. These men say that at the Alcoholics Anonymous meetings they forget to think of themselves as parolees and as such - at least in their own minds - indelibly different from others, because of the kindness and good will of the group. The same spirit of acceptance is manifested by the outside Alcoholics Anonymous groups who come to jails and prisons and participate in group meetings there.

Not only when they are doing well, but also in their fellow members' moments of despair, persons in the Alcoholics Anonymous Fellowship have shown unusual maturity in avoiding the use of blame or condemnation. Their calm and patient acceptance has been of genuine value to their fellows in times of

---

* "Group Work in the Institution", New York, N.Y., Whiteside-Morrow, 1954, page 32.

11

trouble. How much better this world would be for everyone if parents and those who have similar authoritarian functions, such as teachers, welfare workers, and employers, and even religious advisors, realized that their greatest contribution to the lives of those dependent upon them may come from their acceptance with mature objectivity of the troubled and unpleasant behavior of others. Anyone can accept the good achievements of those for whom they have some responsibility. It demands fortitude and maturity to treat without blame or other unfortunate emotional expressions, as do the members of Alcoholics Anonymous, the seeming failure or maladjustment of others.

GROUP COUNSELING IN PRISON PRACTICE:

The use of group interaction in the treatment of offenders in prison is of relatively recent origin. For example, the subject of this book, the program called group counseling, was first explored in the prisons of California in 1944, when it was introduced into the Reception-Guidance Center at San Quentin. Certificated teachers with some training in educational counseling conducted the groups at that time and during subsequent years. A decade later, in 1954, the more extensive program of group counseling, described in this volume, was started. It differs from the earlier program in that in addition to academic teachers the leaders of the groups include vocational instructors, correctional officers, tradesmen, work foremen, clerical workers, and employees in other non-clinical job classifications.

The good reception of group counseling in which these many other kinds of employees participated, was made possible because of a number of supportive developments in the prisons during the previous years. The improved classification of inmates through better diagnosis of their personalities, and so more adequate selections for inclusion in groups, was important in making possible the introduction of group counseling. Advances during the previous decade in general institutional management and in the methods and resources for training and treatment used in the prisons of California, also prepared the viewpoints of inmates and staff for the group counseling program. The emphasis upon the importance of methods of rehabilitation as well as of security in the in-service training program for employees was still another significant factor. These and other advances, which might be mentioned, brought about the kind of institutional climate in which a new program like group counseling might prosper.

A THUMBNAIL SKETCH OF GROUP COUNSELING:

The term group counseling was used to describe the program in California from its beginning with teachers as group leaders in the Reception-Guidance Center in 1944 until the present time when all employees are eligible to be considered for training as group leaders. Other terms for group methods have been used elsewhere, such as group-orientation. A course name like Social Living has been given to discussion groups in some prisons. The more impressive term, guided group interaction, has been used in New Jersey in programs where those conducting groups have had considerable clinical training and also previous experience in group psychotherapy. A greater technical competence is implied among group leaders than that likely to be found in lay employees of prisons and other correctional agencies. In welfare agencies, the terms, worker-clients conference group and worker-clients discussion group have sometimes been mentioned as appropriate terminology for groups conducted by non-clinical personnel.

In group counseling as now conducted in the California prisons, the optimal group has been considered to be about ten or twelve inmates, although in practice some groups are smaller and others larger. The co-leader plan has also been used, when two employees work together in the conduct of a group. The weekly meetings are an hour and a half in length. Groups are conducted in classrooms, vocational training shops, industrial areas, corridors of cell blocks, or other places, sometimes of a makeshift nature, like a storage room. In pleasant weather, foremen of work crews have met with their inmates in some suitable location outdoors.

In general, the procedures are non-directive. What the group discusses is for the most part developed spontaneously by the inmates themselves. However, devices like motion pictures depicting some mental health theme or an invitation to a resource person, such as a psychologist or a parole officer, to attend an occasional session, are also employed to stimulate discussion.

For most of the California prisons and camps, the participation has been from fifty to seventy per cent of the inmate population. There are institutions or honor camps wherein all inmates have agreed, as a condition for transfer there, to attend group counseling. At present, the number actually participating each week in group counseling in the California prisons is the impressive total of about ten thousand inmates and seven hundred employees.

One of the important developments in prison management resulting from the introduction of group counseling has been the giving of recognized treatment roles to the custodial staff. Although for a number of years correctional officers, formerly called prison guards, had been receiving in-service training which described the purpose and values of treatment, nevertheless in actual practice they had remained generally on the fringe of the treatment program. In striking contrast, group counseling is conducted in the California prisons by correctional officers who are the leaders in about sixty per cent of the groups now in operation.

These and other employees, usually men and women

with serious career interests and ambitions in correctional work, were given special training before
being included in the program. After being selected
to participate in the program, group leaders may receive advice and guidance from those who supervise
them in their regular jobs and also from correctional
caseworkers employed on full-time to supervise them.
Other sensible protections, which will be discussed
later, have been thrown around the group counseling
program in the prisons to guide the efforts of the
lay participants and to conserve their interest.

DIFFERENCES BETWEEN GROUP COUNSELING AND GROUP THERAPY:

As for the program itself, one of the first
questions raised by those interested is how group
counseling differs from group psychotherapy, usually
shortened to the term, group therapy. Historically,
group therapy was used earlier than group counseling
in correctional institutions. A significant difference
between the two procedures is the types of workers
involved. In group counseling, an employee of any
classification may be given preparatory training and
approved for participation under supervision. Group
therapy is conducted by psychiatrists, psychologists,
and social workers who are expected to have had some
formal training in guiding therapeutically-oriented
groups. As a form of psychiatric treatment, group
therapy is concerned with more serious emotional problems than group counseling. The methods used may differ because of the greater depth of the emotional
problems treated in group therapy. The number of sessions per week may be more frequent in group therapy
because of the greater complexity of the disturbances
in the inmates treated.

Harrison* has differentiated between group

---

*   Harrison, R.M., "Model for Group Counseling",
    Sacramento, California, Department of Cor-
    rections, 1960, pp. 1-2.

counseling and group therapy, as follows:

> "Group counseling will be most constructive
> when the counselor functions within realistic
> limits of the group counseling program and of
> his own experience and training. In general,
> counselors can be expected to listen, mode-
> rate, draw out diverse feelings and points of
> view, reflect feelings, help evaluate past
> and present experiences and future goals. It
> is not valid to expect group counselors to
> probe into unconscious areas, or to make dy-
> namic interpretations in order to resolve
> unconscious conflicts."

Certain types of serious offenders, for example,
habitual criminals with deep-seated problems of long
standing need group psychotherapy. Group counseling,
conducted by laymen, has as its goal, to quote Harrison
again, "not major personality change but rather the
development of latent strengths in the offender through
healthy and constructive human relations." Harrison
also commented in this regard, that "group counseling can be likened to good nursing care." And, he
added that "some therapists have reported that group
counseling may be a good preparation for group therapy in some cases."*

For many offenders, the amount of change in personality adjustment to transform them from criminality
to ordinarily acceptable citizenship is not great,
according to Dr. H. Michael Rosow, the psychiatric
consultant to the Los Angeles Out-Patient Clinic of
the Division of Adult Parolees.** These offenders

---

* The above are quotations from a letter to the
author under date of January 20th, 1961.

** A point made by Dr. Rosow during a Seminar at
the California Institution for Men at Chino
on December 7, 1955.

may achieve through group counseling growth toward
at least the minimal wholesomeness of personality
necessary for law-abiding life in the community. But
offenders with seriously damaged personalities need
more intensive treatment which involves deeper emotional levels than those which may suitably be dealt
with in group counseling. Obviously, the greater
clinical knowledge and experience of the psychother-
apist and his more intensive methods of treatment
are necessary to understand and to treat the minority of offenders who are not included in Dr. Rosow's
classification.

STUDIES CONCERNING GROUP COUNSELING:

At present, research studies* are being conducted to evaluate the group counseling program. In
general, the preliminary findings are favorable as
regards the effects upon the conduct of the participants and the morale of the institution. The adjustment of counselees as a group within the institution is better, and the proportion of escapes less,
than what has been recorded for those not in group
counseling. Some of these studies, which are difficult to conduct scientifically because of the many
variables involved, have nevertheless had fairly
satisfactory control groups. The morale of the staff
in an institution with one hundred per cent inmate
participation in group counseling was reported as
definitely superior to that found in the other fa-

---

* One of the most extensive studies is a five-year
research project begun in 1958 at the University
of California at Los Angeles under a subsidy of
about two thousand dollars from the National
Institute for Mental Health of the United States
Public Health Service. The Research Division of
the California Department of Corrections under
the dynamic leadership of J. Douglas Grant has
many interesting and valuable studies now in
process and plans for others soon to be started.

cilities in the prison system. Of course, other factors - for example, its smaller size - undoubtedly also contributed to this high morale rating. These studies are being repeated with more- adequate controls. But even if the above mentioned results were discounted greatly, they would still suggest that group counseling has made a valuable contribution to institutional operation.

The initial introduction and subsequent development of group counseling in the prisons, although supported and encouraged by the central administration in Sacramento, was left for decision to the local institutional leadership. Before enlargement in each of the institutions the program was subjected to considerable critical study by the warden and his top staff. Since 1954 when group counseling was first tried in its present form, institutional participation has increased greatly, so that at present about one half of the inmates in the California prison system are enrolled in the program. This expansion of the application of group counseling is impressive, however, it offers in itself no final proof as to the value of group counseling in correctional practice.

The findings for the comparative post-release adjustment of counselees compared with others on parole or discharge are encouraging, though in general not startling. Harrison* has noted that "we have clearer evidence of the contributions of group counseling to the safe operation of the prison than we do, as yet, for long-term rehabilitative benefit." An exception is found in the surprisingly high rate of satisfactory adjustment on parole of men from what are called "long-term, low turnover" groups, conducted with the same inmates for a year or more under the same competent and dedicated leaders. Clearly positive

---

*   Harrison, R.M., "Mental Health Applications in the California Correctional System", The Chatham Conference, Boston University, 1960, page 61.

results in the form of unusually good records on parole have been reported in follow-up studies of those
who attended such groups while in the institution.
These favorable findings are being subjected to rigor-
ous review and additional studies have been planned
by the Research Division of the Department of Corrections and by other groups.

A major value reported in various observations
and studies has been the improvement in communication
between inmates and staff.* The long-established
separation, as though in two different cultures, of
inmates and employees seems to be much less evident.
More good will toward each other is expressed by the
human beings in the institution. For example, early
returns from a study in a reformatory-type institution
indicate a decrease in hostility and in gang behavior
there after group counseling had been introduced.
According to comments of the staff, the general emotional climate of the place seemed to have improved.

In an investigation at San Quentin, Roberts reported that** "The data suggest a change among group
counseling inmates from an attitude indicative of
strict compliance with or adherence to the prescrip-
tions of the inmate social system, to one indicating
a lesser degree of acceptance of these traditional
controls. Also suggested, in the responses of the
counselees, was a greater degree of acceptance in
their social relationship with other individuals
and races. "

---

* See the statement by Grant, J.D., "The Research
  Newsletter", 1960, March, pages 1-2.

** Roberts, E.L.R., "A Study of the Effects of Group
  Counseling on Association Choices and Status
  Ascription among inmates at the California State
  Prison at San Quentin", Master's Thesis, San
  Francisco State College, 1960, page 75.

19

Another possible contribution of group counseling that has been reported is the growth in the interest of custodial officers in their work, accompanied by greater belief in the desirability of treatment for prisoners.* The reason the program has sometimes been called revolutionary is due to these changes in the attitudes and activities of inmates and the rank and file of institutional employees. These seem to contradict any dogmatic viewpoint that the prison community is by its very nature irreparably divided into the two irreconcilable cultures, the one of the inmates, and the other of the staff. On the contrary, these preliminary studies suggest that when group counseling is effective, there may be not only better co-existence but the beginning of more genuine communication and cooperation between inmates and staff.

THE USE OF SUBJECTIVE EVALUATIONS:

In the appraisal of the values of group counseling in this volume, we will need to rely upon subjective judgments as well as objective demonstrations. Obviously, studies of programs which deal with human beings cannot be carried out with the exact analyses and controls used in the physical sciences. Groups of people cannot be subjected to such rigid conditions. The multiplicity of factors involved in studying, for example, the changes in the emotional climate of an institution, makes it necessary to depend to some extent upon intuition and other non-intellectual sources of judgment to describe what seems to be happening. Even if every effort were made to translate these deeply-felt opinions more nearly into the kind of validity associated with the physical sciences, our efforts would still fall short of the exactitude of the statistical ideal.

---

* Preliminary findings from the research study directed by J.W. Eaton conducted at the University of California at Los Angeles and mentioned earlier.

Many persons who have lived in institutions before and after group counseling was introduced are deeply convinced that group counseling brings about desirable changes in the human relationships and in the atmosphere or the emotional climate of these places. If not demonstrably attributable to group counseling, these advances are perceived by many as at least concomitant therewith. Some also have intuitive convictions which lead them to go further and to consider group counseling to be of causal significance, in conjunction with other advances in correctional work, in bringing about this change for the better in the general tone of correctional institutions.

The reader is forewarned that subjective evaluations enter actively into upholding the values of group counseling. Incidentally, one may also expect the use of subjective data in support of the objections of those who may oppose group counseling. Intuitive convictions are admittedly influential in the minds of those who believe in the usefulness of the program in correctional institutions. However, these subjective evaluations are supported whenever possible by findings based on orthodox research methods and procedures. In recent years, those in positions of leadership in the group counseling program in the California Department of Corrections have strongly encouraged and supported requests to foundations for funds to evaluate group counseling objectively in institutional practice. As some of these have been granted, additional objective studies will be completed before too long and, we hope, answer more satisfactorily many questions concerning the values of group counseling.

SUMMARY OF THE CHAPTER:

In recent years, the influences of group interaction upon human personality have been the subject of many studies in the social sciences. After the constructive effects of human interrelationships were

21

recognized, persons engaged in correctional and welfare work began to experiment with their use in the treatment of inmates and other clients. One of the outcomes of such exploration has been group psychotherapy. Another, the subject of this volume, has been group counseling.

On the basis of favorable findings as to its use in prisons and honor camps, group counseling has been considered for application and has also been tried in other places. However, before it is introduced anywhere, its limitations must be understood; the minimal necessities for its effective operation assured. Some of the prerequisites have been mentioned in this chapter. These and other considerations in the use of group counseling will be discussed at greater length later in the book.

Future research, we hope, may evaluate more clearly whatever values group counseling may have in contributing toward a reduction in recidivism, the primary concern of penologists. In several studies, group counseling has been reported as making contributions of value to institutional management, such as the improved orderliness and general atmosphere or morale of a prison.

One of the most significant contributions of group counseling has been the enlistment in the treatment program of correctional officers, shop foremen, vocational instructors, members of the clerical staff, and other employees not usually identified with institutional therapeutic efforts. This may, indeed, be one of its greatest contributions. Through improved inmate-staff communication and other advantages, group counseling may pave the way for future progress in the conversion of correctional institutions into places where helpful treatment is expected by those who are sent there.

CHAPTER 2

PRACTICAL CONSIDERATIONS IN THE USE OF GROUP COUNSELING

EMOTIONAL ATTITUDES TOWARD TREATMENT:

It is not easy to be objective in thinking about criminals. Especially when a crime has involved violence, brutality, or the abuse of children, the normal person is moved by feelings of shocked revulsion, amounting sometimes to hatred and rage. In every one the quality of the emotional reaction to crime is different; we all have our individual sensitivities. Thus one person is especially indignant over theft or destruction of property, another is exceedingly shocked by a crime involving needless brutality, and most of us are hurt and revolted by an instance in which a child is injured physically or lured into the use of narcotics. However natural these feelings may be, they do not advance and may seriously retard plans for the rehabilitation of the criminal.

The modern penologist is primarily interested in enabling the offender to overcome his antisocial behavior. This means that adequate treatment in prison commensurate with the needs of the prisoner is more important than is a kind or degree of punishment that accords with the amount and quality of the anger or revulsion that might be aroused by his crime.

Chief Justice Earl Warren* has clearly offered in the following quotation the several choices before the American people in regard to what generally

---

* "The Public Papers of Chief Justice Earl Warren", New York, Simon & Shuster, 1959, page 20.

speaking may be done to those who violate the law:

> "The idea of punishment has not and cannot be entirely abandoned. It should, however, be regarded as only one of the many possible devices for discipline, treatment and ultimate rehabilitation. The protection of society, both immediately and ultimately is conceived to be the primary purpose of a system of criminal justice. It is obvious that the ultimate protection of society can be achieved in only three ways - by the imposition of the death penalty, by confinement for life or by reformation.
>
> In the practical administration of criminal law, more than 95% of all convicted offenders are ultimately released. The dictates of logic demand, therefore, that every resource at our disposal be directed toward the re-education and regeneration of offenders in order that they may eventually assume the responsibilities of citizenship."

Whatever may be the conflict in the feelings of correctional workers toward the offender, one practical consideration, emphasized by Chief Justice Warren, should never be forgotten. An overwhelmingly large percentage of offenders return to society from jail or prison. The need for an adequate program of rehabilitation for them is of grave social importance.

Just as there may be adverse emotional attitudes towards offenders among correctional workers so, likewise, is it to be noted that welfare workers also experience conflicting feelings over what they would like to see happen to some kinds of clients. Examples are those who are extremely ungrateful and uncooperative, or the minority of seemingly dishonest persons, who while receiving public or private assistance, behave in dishonorable ways. These kinds of clients may arouse feelings of disgust or resentment among those in welfare work. As correctional workers need to differentiate the crime from the offender and to deal with the latter as an individual in need of treatment, so also must the welfare worker try to separate these unpleasant characteristics of some of their clients from their need for service. Competence in behaving thus objectively may be one measure of the worker's maturity.

OBSTACLES IN INTRODUCING GROUP COUNSELING:

The unfortunate consequences of the worker's own disturbed feelings toward the attitudes and behavior of a minority of clients may be a less readily recognized handicap in conducting group counseling. There are a number of other obstacles in the way of starting group counseling which are more obvious and practical. These interferences need to be realized in advance by those contemplating its introduction. In the first place, there may be physical barriers. The group counseling program requires a relatively quiet room for best results. Some agencies have no suitable places in which to conduct group counseling. In the jails, for example, the inmate dining room or sometimes a small chapel or a visiting room may be suggested. However, the dining room may not be available until well after the evening meal. The chapel may involve obstacles because of institutional policy since, for example, smoking may not be permitted there. Ordinarily, the group counseling sessions are informal occasions during which smoking has been permitted. Security precautions may forbid the use of the visiting room at night, even if it were suitable.

In the future, let us hope, the architecture of jails and prisons will change to accommodate advances in penology. In the years ahead, if the program proves to be of value, facilities for group counseling will need to be included in the original

25

plans for the construction of these facilities. Until then, the program will have to be accommodated to existent limited facilities as has been true in the prisons.

Allied to the absence of places to hold the sessions, is a second and even more prohibitive obstacle, the lack of staff to conduct the groups. Employees who are interested, willing, and potentially competent as group leaders, may not be free to participate because of other important obligations. If a jailer has an entire floor to supervise, including several dormitories or tanks in which groups of men are confined, obviously he cannot be spared to conduct a group, because while doing so he would be unable to observe what is going on in the other parts of the jail for whose operation he is responsible. Likewise, during a period of serious unemployment, the workers in a social agency may be so swamped by the increase in their caseloads that time may not seem to be available for conducting groups.

In some institutions or agencies, the lack of available staff seems to be a serious practical obstacle to introducing group counseling. In others adjustments have been made to overcome this handicap. The most satisfactory means of providing staff time for group counseling is by developing the means to integrate the operation into the regular duties of employees. Some of the prisons have instituted a weekly group counseling hour to enable employees to conduct the program on regular state time. Another suitable arrangement has been to pay regular employees overtime for conducting groups.

The inability to provide adequate supervision for the program of group counseling may be a third obstacle. An important requirement, if group counseling is to prosper, is the provision of supervision for the lay leaders. In each of the California prisons there is at least one correctional caseworker with some training in clinical psychology or social

26

work employed for this purpose on a full-time basis. After the initial demonstrations and discussions, in-service instruction in group methods and other relevant matters are continued for the group leaders by these supervisors. The firsthand observation by these experienced correctional caseworkers of the actual conduct of the groups by the laymen involved has also been essential to the program. For purposes of additional instruction, it is desirable to have available the services of resource persons with training in the clinical areas such as psychiatry, psychology or psychiatric social work. However, those beginning a program of group counseling may be interested to know that the supervision of group counseling in the California prisons was makeshift at first and developed in quality with the growth of the program. It is still in need of much improvement to meet all the major needs of the laymen who conduct groups.

A fourth obstacle in the conduct of group counseling is concerned with the human factors which may undermine the long-term effectiveness of any institutional or agency operation. There are, for example, varying moods among the participants. Thus, a program may start with great interest and enthusiasm. A number of staff members may be courageously and hopefully involved. As the novelty wears off and the demands for greater patience and effort enter, among them may occur doubts, disappointments or discouragements. Then, even those originally most enthusiastic have serious fluctuations of attitudes and feelings which may prompt in them questions as their own competence to conduct group counseling or even doubts of the values of the program itself. However, variations in mood are characteristic of many if not most human enterprises. They must not be given too much weight in evaluating the basic values of any program. The importance of good supervision, however, becomes apparent if these human problems are to be met when they arise as promptly as necessary.

27

The above discussion of obstacles preventing the introduction of group counseling emphasizes the importance of the interest and support of top management. The leadership in an institution or agency, when sympathetically and understandingly interested in group counseling, can usually make adjustments of staff and consultant resources to further its operation. If the administrators themselves are fearful or skeptical, any of the above obstacles may then serve as a valid excuse for postponing the introduction of group counseling. The absence of genuine administrative support may be an insuperable obstacle preventing an adequate trial of group counseling, or many other programs that might be considered for use.

STAFF TRAINING IN GROUP COUNSELING:

Experience during the past seven years has led to the definition of what is desirable by way of employee preparation before participation in group counseling. Those who desire to take part in the program should first attend at least eight successive weekly sessions of a demonstration group developed anew for the purpose of demonstration, and conducted by an experienced group leader. For those interested in knowing what group counseling is, no substitute can take the place of the actual, first-hand observation of the conduct of a group. It is interesting that during these demonstration sessions the group of inmates or other clients have usually not been inhibited by the presence of visitors for whose presence they have been carefully prepared, so that the visitor gets a fairly adequate impression of the natural and usual character of a group session.

The inmates or other clients leave after each of these demonstration periods. Subsequently those who have attended as trainees may spend at least half an hour with the group leader in the discussion of what went on during the session. Explanations may be given by the instructor and questions may be raised by the trainees. These discussions, supplemented by the reading of an elementary text prepared for their use should acquaint the trainees with the general purposes and some of the details of the operation of group counseling. In some agencies, an initial orientation lecture conducted before the first demonstration session has been valuable.

If resources permit, before being assigned his own group, the trainee should also participate in a few sessions of a group being conducted regularly by a colleague experienced in group counseling, wherein perhaps the trainee may be permitted to function as co-leader. The group leader should have time after each session to discuss with the trainee matters of interest or concern. If the trainee qualifies and is assigned a group, his initial conduct of the group should be supervised by an experienced caseworker. The supervisor should also conduct regularly scheduled classes for the further training of group leaders.

Obviously, an administrator would increase the preparatory training program in accordance with the organization's resources. The measures suggested here compromise a minimal pattern of desirable training. Each agency would have to adjust the program for training group leaders in accordance with its institutional resources and the professional backgrounds of the members of the staff. Likewise, supervision and staff development may be planned in terms of the best use of regional resources in the nature of college courses or other adult educational services.

THE MORALE OF THE GROUP LEADER:
All groups have much in common but no two of them would be identical. These variations among groups may be expected in view of the differing backgrounds of the group leaders. Differences in

the personalities of group leaders make for a variety of acceptable methods of conducting groups. Although there can be no standardized or uniform way of handling a group, there are some procedures, like the use of motion pictures, that can be carried out with some similarity by all group leaders. In others, such as the use of non-directive procedures, some group leaders may have greater natural ability and may require less instruction than others. Those who supervise the program must recognize these individual differences in capacity and adaptability among group leaders and plan their work accordingly with them as individuals.

In addition to instruction in methodology, the supervisor must also keep in mind the importance of the morale of the group leader. His patience, calm assurance and expectation of constructive outcomes in his group, when conducted for a period of weeks or months, are of primary importance. A basic function of the supervisor is accordingly to help the group leader to retain his interest and hopefulness, especially during the difficult beginning months.

Although some extraordinary changes have occurred in inmates in group counseling, there are few if any miracles. This is true, as the reader is well aware, of other methods of treatment. Moreover, the conduct of group counseling is not easy. The group leader must not become disheartened by the many difficulties and sources of discouragement which come to everyone in this field. For that matter, demands upon the maturity of the group leader are not unlike those made in their work with other persons upon teachers or even specialists in psychiatry or psychology.

The supervisor, therefore, has an obligation to encourage the group leaders under his guidance to express their feelings about their work as group leaders, especially during these expected periods of insecurity or discouragement. In this connection, supervisors have found it valuable to conduct for the group leaders assigned to them for guidance, sessions which in essence resemble group counseling. The basic challenge confronting the supervisor of group counseling might perhaps be summarized as helping the newly appointed group leader to transform his initial eagerness and his colorful expectations into what might be described as patient and informed optimism.

INFORMATION FOR THE LEADER ABOUT HIS GROUP:

The group leader needs to have some understanding of the backgrounds and problems of those in his group. In agencies like probation departments or welfare offices, the personnel have access to the case files. After instruction in the importance of confidentiality, it would be very desirable for group leaders in correctional institutions, if they so desire, to have access to the case history.

One must at this point raise the moot question, "Does the administration of the institution consider its employees mature enough to be trusted with confidential information?" Not only is this a question within an agency, but doubts regarding confidentiality have also been raised among social agencies in the exchange of case material. Similarly, in child guidance work in the schools, administrators have been heard to voice their doubts as to the ability of teachers to treat as confidential any clinical information they may receive about children and their families. School administrators are afraid that teachers will be guilty of gossiping about what they learn from the case records. One experience seems to contradict this belief. Over a period of a decade, state traveling child guidance clinics* working in many hundreds of schools

---

* Fenton, N. and Wallace, R., "State Child Guidance Services in California Communities", Sacramento, California, Supervisor of Documents, 1938, 157 pp.

and with thousands of teachers confirmed that with very infrequent exceptions, teachers, when properly prepared, were as respecting of confidential material as are clinicians, lawyers, or other professional people.

Experiences in the prisons have also confirmed the trustworthiness of non-clinical* employees regarding the confidential material in the case history, when the importance of confidentiality has been fully explained to them. These employees include career correctional or welfare workers who possess a valuable background of work experience though they lack the advanced academic training, especially graduate work in a university, which professional specialists have in the fields of psychiatry, psychology or social work. Many of these employees may, however, be rather widely read in general or professional literature. Many have themselves had experiences in social living making for maturity and dependability in matters of confidentiality. It should be noted, however, that they need not necessarily be informed of all the material on file if it includes items of a highly classified character. Thus, personnel in the prisons would not have access to what has been called figuratively the "hot file" where information of a highly confidential and even dangerous nature is kept.

Personnel in correctional institutions and agencies need to be trained and encouraged to study the case histories of those with whom they are concerned. What better use can one think of for case histories, so very costly in their preparation, than

---

* In this volume, the term non-clinical is preferred over non-professional in differentiating personnel. Many of the leaders in group counseling belong to professions such as teaching, or deserve to be called professional because of studious application and long experience in correctional work.

that their findings be used by those who are involved responsibly in the treatment of inmates and other clients.

SUMMARY: THE OPEN MIND TOWARD A NEW PROGRAM:

The purpose of this chapter is to give administrators and workers in welfare and correctional agencies some rather general ideas regarding the introduction of group counseling. From these, it is believed, they may more easily and comfortably determine whether or not they wish to introduce the program. Much needs to be done to overcome some of the present barriers, physical and psychological, to conducting group counseling in the jails and other county detention facilities. Limitations may also be present to interfere with its conduct with probationers or welfare recipients in the community. Among these obstacles may be physical barriers, such as no adequate place to meet, or staff limitations, the lack of employees available to conduct or supervise groups. There may also be psychological obstacles because of the emphasis upon conservative practices and ideas in the institution or agency. Again, the worker, secure in individual casework, may be threatened by the group approach and be fearful of trying it.

In the prisons, group counseling has been a cooperative enterprise in which all employees were considered eligible to participate. In most of the institutions, the associate wardens and others of the upper echelons of the staff have also conducted groups. Generally, the participants have had an overall interest in the program. When the program started, they felt themselves to be partners in getting group counseling under way and in facilitating its advancement.

Much of the opposition to group counseling in the prisons has come from those who did not participate in the training program and had little or no firsthand knowledge of its nature and purposes. There were some opponents who thought group counseling might interfere with their authoritarian control over the inmates. Others were opposed because of the administrative and budgetary problems accompanying the introduction of a new program. In contrast to this latter type of opposition to group counseling was the favorable action following their observation of actual groups in one of the prisons by upper echelon officials concerned with the California state budget. These highly conservative persons were sufficiently impressed by what they observed to recognize the need for and to recommend the appropriation by the legislature of funds for the compensation of officers conducting groups on their own time.

Because of possible obstacles or resistance, group counseling should be introduced slowly and carefully. The program should be developed with as much voluntary participation as possible. It should be adapted to the nature and purposes of the institution or agency and to the type of clientele served. Thus, the staff of a probation department or a welfare agency, after their observations of group counseling in action, should explore its possibilities and define the conditions under which it might be introduced into their own operation. Once begun, the program should be given sufficient time under patient and critical auspices before making any comprehensive evaluations as to its usefulness.

In the study of group counseling and in its application, open-mindedness is important. To praise the program too enthusiastically or, on the contrary, to oppose it with a mind almost closed by the formula "it can't be done", so characteristic of conservatives everywhere, are both ill-advised. Rather the reader should try to approach group counseling with the objectivity or healthy skepticism of the open mind.

CHAPTER 3

THE LAYMAN PARTICIPATES IN THE TREATMENT PROGRAM

WHAT IS MEANT BY TREATMENT IN PRISON:

In recent decades, simultaneously with the advancement of methods of diagnosis in delinquency and criminality and in public assistance programs and other social services, has come the development of methods of treatment. With the expansion of treatment programs in these areas of service has come the need to survey and to define legitimate boundaries for the treatment activities and responsibilities of the different specialties, notably psychiatry, clinical psychology and social work, and also to consider how and where the so-called non-clinical employees may participate.

At the time group counseling was introduced, the point of view toward treatment that prevailed in the prisons of California was defined in a book prepared for all employees to read as part of their required in-service training. It was released before the group counseling program started. The following statement on page 10 of this official In-Service Training Manual* presents a broad concept of institutional treatment:

"Whatever is done in the prison to or for the inmate is treatment. What is done may by helpful or it may be harmful, as regard

---

* Fenton, N., "An Introduction to Classification and Treatment in State Correctional Service", with a Foreword by Richard A. McGee. Sacramento, California, Department of Corrections, 1953, 192 pp.

35

the individual's progress toward becoming a better person. When an officer does anything to an inmate, gives him an order, observes his work, makes a gesture toward him, or even just gives him a glance, - something happens between them which may be helpful or harmful. Usually, these relationships affect the inmate's personality in some way or other and therefore may be considered to be treatment. The correctional officer and others must realize that what we call treatment goes on everywhere in the prisons. It is not confined merely to places like the medical clinic, the school room or the chaplain's office. The correctional officer, including the man in the tower, may have a part for good or ill in treatment."

IS GROUP COUNSELING TREATMENT?

It is obvious from the above quotation that group counseling has been a part of institutional treatment in the California prisons. This may be demonstrated by the following reports, which could be amplified by countless others, of what actually occurred in two counseling groups:

During the initial weeks of a counseling group at the Folsom State Prison, the fifteen inmates involved, all of them with previous prison records, manifested great hostility in speaking about their parole agents. They complained especially of unfairness in being sent back to prison. This type of hostile expression continued during several sessions. Persons in law enforcement were also criticized. About the third or fourth session, one of the men said: "Let's quit this blaming others for our being here. So far as I'm concerned, and if you quit kidding yourselves this also goes for most of you, I'm the one who is responsible for my being here. Me and no one else! My parole agent gave me every possible break. He tried hard to keep me out but I just couldn't make it. So let's look at the real cause of our being here, ourselves, and quit blaming others." Murmurs of assent and other evidence of agreement came from others in the group.

The group leader did not enter into the discussion. He permitted the hostilities to be expressed without protesting. Probably, the inmates themselves through the group interaction were able to arrive at a more readily accepted explanation of and adjustment to their feelings toward parole agents and other authority figures than might have come about if the group leader had tried to lecture to them or had expostulated to them about the errors in their attitudes toward these persons in authority. It is evident that something of value happened to at least a few of the men in the group to change somewhat their attitudes toward persons in authority. This change or growth in the counselees may . reasonably be regarded as an outcome of correctional treatment.

A second actual incident illustrates how inmates help one another to get a better understanding of themselves. In a group in the California Institution for Men at Chino, an inmate complained that everybody picked on him. Even that very day an officer had reprimanded him especially sharply. The officer, he declared, like everyone else, had it in for him. After he had gone on with this sort of talk for a while, another inmate asked him: "Do you really want to know why this happens to you?" The first man replied that he did. The second inmate then said: "You ask for it. You always go around with a chip on your shoulder, something always seems to be eating you." Another inmate spoke up and said: "I saw what happened with you and the officer today, and if I had been him, I'd have spoken a hell of a lot sharper that he did. You had it coming to you. Why don't you get wise to yourself?" These remarks were spoken rather roughly but with evident kindly intention.

37

The group had been meeting for several weeks and morale was good. After some further give-and-take in the group, during which the inmate fought back, he finally agreed that maybe he was touchy and explained it by reference to worry over his wife and children. Although attentive to what was said, the group leader did not participate in the discussion. The other inmates were able to encourage the man who had seemingly begun, albeit reluctantly, to recognize his problem.

These two examples indicate how in well conducted groups the inmates discuss their problems and react to each other. Evidently constructive outcomes may and do result from group counseling sessions. It is also obvious that this can justifiably be called correctional treatment.

TREATMENT AS A CONTINUUM:

The treatment of human beings with troublesome problems of various sorts may be regarded as a continuum. At one end are the routine daily contacts with clients like those quoted above from the Departmental Training Manual. What goes on in these everyday contacts may influence the attitudes and behavior of inmates for better or for worse. At the other end of the continuum are the most technical forms of psychotherapy, well beyond the purview of the layman. To the question, "Where can the layman participate constructively in the treatment program?", the answer can be no sharp line of demarcation applicable to all institutions and agencies. For one thing their participation would be defined by the concept of institutional organization and management that directs or governs the work of the particular agency.

If our prisons are really to be treatment-oriented, then the whole staff must participate in

treatment. Maxwell Jones and Harry A. Wilmer in
their important books* have described mental hospitals conducted in accordance with the concept of
institutional management called the therapeutic community. Both stress the values in the treatment program of the entire staff. The eminent psychiatrist
Karl Menninger is quoted on page 12 of an important
contribution to modern institutional management**
as placing great emphasis upon what he has called
milieu therapy. He is quoted therein on page 12 as
saying that "even the person who swept the floor
might be the very one able to give a particular patient the kind of psychological help needed." The
point of view stressed by these outstanding psychiatric authorities has been helpful in the current
thinking of penologists. Today, only the most ob-
tuse or naive clinician in mental hospitals or prisons would raise any question regarding the participation in treatment of the entire staff. From the
positive viewpoint, as Menninger believes, "every
individual who came in contact with patients" has
potentialities for helpful treatment and should
when possible be used in the institutional program.

As already noted, just where group counseling
would be located on the hypothetical treatment continuum is not a well defined location. For one thing,
group counseling would vary in effectiveness with
the dedication and competence of the group leader.

---

*   Jones, M. et al, "The Therapeutic Community",
     New York, N.Y., Basic Books, 1953, 186 pp.
     Wilmer, H.A., "Social Psychiatry in Action -
     A Therapeutic Community", Springfield, Illinois,
     Charles C. Thomas, 1958, 373 pp.

**   Greenblatt, M., York, R.N., and Brown, E.L.,
     "From Custodial to Therapeutic Care in Mental
     Hospitals", New York, N.Y., Russell Sage
     Foundation, 1955, 497 pp.

Thus, one group, because of the inadequacy or in-experience of the leader, might be superficial in character and not affect the inmates significantly as regards their rehabilitation. Another group conducted over many months by a dedicated, skillful and well trained group leader might, as preliminary studies have indicated, be of considerable value for the rehabilitation of the men in the group. Therefore the most plausible answer would locate group counseling on the continuum of correctional treatment from above the most superficial level to somewhere short of the point where highly technical, clinically-oriented group psychotherapy would begin.

CRITERIA IN THE ADMINISTRATION OF THE PROGRAM:

Three basic considerations may be noted in the conduct of a treatment program which includes the participation of laymen. All are concerned with the understanding of the nature and purposes of group counseling by those chosen to participate in the program. Related thereto are descriptions and explanations of the resources for the assistance and direction of those who are selected to lead groups. The first consideration would be the definition of what the non-clinical employees may be permitted to do. The second is the provision of clearly defined measures for administrative direction and control of their work. And the third would be concerned with the implementation of the second through the provision of adequate supervision of their activities with inmates and other clients.

In the California prison system, in a specially prepared Manual, released by the Director of Corrections, the policies regarding the nature of the participation of laymen in group counseling are defined. The relationships of group counseling to the institutional organization and the administration of the Department are also given. Minimal provisions regarding the supervision of the program are spelled out. The Manual of Policies and Procedures for Group

Counseling was prepared collaboratively by administrators, clinicians and others to establish the above three criteria for the conduct of the program. First, the purposes and limitations of group counseling are defined therein. For example, the differences between group counseling and group psychotherapy are presented. Second, the administrative control of the group counseling program is covered by specific directions concerning its operation. Third, the desirable supervision of the program is carefully defined including the functions of employees appointed to the several new positions that had been established. The supervision of group counseling is directed by the Departmental Supervisor on the Sacramento staff* and local supervisors in each of the California prisons. The latter, correctional caseworkers with advanced training in clinical psychology or social case work, are employed on a full-time basis. Two examples of the responsibilities of these supervisors listed in the Manual are to visit groups and to conduct training sessions for group leaders. To further reinforce the supervision of group counseling in the institutions, psychologists, psychiatrists and social workers have been brought into the program as resource persons in in-service training.

The above is an outline of the general plan of administration of group counseling in the California prisons and honor camps. Progress in its accomplishment has been encouraging. However, much more needs to be done before all the many details are accomplished in institutional practice.

---

* Robert M. Harrison, the first to be appointed to this position, is a psychiatric social worker with wide experience in group methods of treatment, including the use therein of laymen in mental hospitals and in military organizations.

41

CHANGES IN THE FUNCTIONS OF CORRECTIONAL EMPLOYEES:

Group counseling has provided new functions for correctional workers of many job classifications. The older, more conventional duties and activities of correctional officers, teachers, maintenance foremen and other employees have been enhanced by their participation in treatment. This has also led to a closer association with the clinical specialists on the staff and more receptive and understanding attitudes toward their work. For their part, many institutional psychologists, psychiatrists and social workers have revised their attitudes toward the non-clinical persons on the staff. To accord with the new institutional climate which has evolved from group counseling they have also modified some of their procedures in treating inmates.

Clinicians have found that laymen on the staff can contribute much of value to strengthen what they themselves are attempting to do for the inmates. Figuratively, the pilot house of the treatment program may still be the clinical center. The actual points of contact of the treatment program will, however, be recognized as including all other places where inmates are in personal relationship with employees.

The attention of the clinical specialists has thereby been drawn forcibly to the need to obtain the cooperation of all employees if their efforts are to be of greatest potential value. Similar changes in staff relationships will also occur in the correctional or social agency in the community with the advancement in the treatment program that may accompany the introduction of group counseling.

This change in institutional and agency outlook should lead eventually to a new type of employee in institutional and community correctional and social agencies, the treatment worker. Persons included in the top management will have to reorient their attitudes toward subordinate employees, respecting, accepting and advancing them in terms of their capacity to relate to inmates or other clients constructively as do human beings of good will toward one another elsewhere. Capacity for entering a constructive relationship with inmates or other clients is the practical essence of what must be required of all employees, if they are to be of. use in the rehabilitation program of the future.

THE ACCEPTANCE OF LIMITS:

What has been said in the previous pages should not be interpreted to suggest that custodial care and precautions regarding the prevention of disorders or escapes are cast aside or disregarded by correctional workers. On the contrary, definite limits of discussion and behavior are required to be maintained by the group leaders. The group meetings must be reasonably orderly. The staff needs to be acutely aware of the present and future significance of social control through the willingness of clients to accept limits to their conduct within the group and elsewhere. It is believed that the understanding of the need for rules and regulations thrashed out in the group results in a greater acceptance of these limits to conduct. Experience thus far has shown, confirmed in an encouraging measure by statistical reports, that the results of group counseling in the prisons tend to accord with this optimistic hypothesis. Early returns from studies of institutional or community living indicate that rules are obeyed by counselees as a group in greater proportion and presumably with better feelings toward their observance than is true of non-counselees.

The great difference between the good hospital and the prison or other correctional agency is the expectation by patients in the former that they may look forward to good results from the treatment they are receiving or will receive. Inmates or parolees are beginning to feel that they are profiting from

the program of correctional treatment, whether it
be academic or vocational training, individual or
group psychotherapy, religious guidance, or group
counseling. It is hopefully anticipated that some
day, as group counseling and these other kinds of
treatment advance, men in correctional facilities
and on parole or probation will have the same attitudes toward the staff, the same security in expecting helpful treatment, as do patients in a general hospital or any other good institution; or as
do clients in the best community clinical or welfare agencies.

SUMMARY OF THE CHAPTER:

To conserve the values of lay participation in
the group counseling program, headquarter's staff
of the California Department of Corrections prepared
a manual which outlines the policies and procedures
concerning group counseling. Satisfactory direction,
control and supervision of the program has been possible because of the adherence to this official definition of its operation by those in charge of institutional management and because of the conscien-
tiousness of the group leaders.

It is to the credit of the local and Departmental
leadership that in selecting and training group leaders and in their direction and supervision, nothing
has occurred in the counseling groups which is un-
suitable from a psychiatric viewpoint, such as incidents of so-called acting-out behavior, or seriously disturbing emotional outbursts. However, many
administrative problems need still to be met. Fore-
most are how to improve the physical conditions
for group meetings, how to plan for additional assistance from the professional clinical staff, how
to provide more participation by the middle management in custody and training and above all, how to

develop more carefully planned supervision and in-service instruction for the group leaders. Compared with most prison programs, like academic or vocational education, group counseling is relatively new. Although the program is progressing, a longer time will be required before its operation attains the necessary administrative maturity.

CHAPTER 4

THE CONDUCT OF GROUP COUNSELING

TWO BASIC REQUIREMENTS FOR GROUP COUNSELING:

When group counseling is being considered as
part of the operation of any organization those interested may begin their studies by noting two basic
conditions which are prerequisite to its adequate
development. One cannot, however, consider these
prerequisite conditions without also bringing in the
closely related objectives of the program. So that
the desiderata for the conduct of group counseling
outlined in this chapter include not only basic requirements but also the accomplishment of certain
objectives for the effective operation of the program.

The first requirement is <u>the development of the
group setting necessary for clients to feel free to
discuss with security their own and each other's
feelings and attitudes toward the situation in which
they find themselves.</u> This may be accomplished if
the group leader is able to accept the inmates or
other clients with sincere interest in their welfare,
to accept them for what they are without experiencing
the discomfort of conflicting attitudes about them
as offenders. The clients after a time recognize the
genuineness of the worker's acceptance and begin to
feel free to say what is on their minds or in their
hearts. The good group may offer for some inmates
concerned with their own reformation, a kind of sanc-
tuary or refuge from the callous environment of the
prison yard.

Group membership in prison, as in any other society, is an important index of social attitudes
and adjustment. Individuals or sub-groups tend to

set standards which, if not universally accepted by the larger group, are at least not openly opposed by them. These standards may be of different levels of social desirability. In the prison the standards set by inmate leaders, described by Clemmer, Sykes, McCorkle and Korn and others, contain elements of a destructive or less desirable nature from the standpoint of rehabilitation. A major contribution of group counseling has been that it permits those with more desirable and constructive attitudes to bring their influence to bear, at least in the groups.

Clemmer in his classic study, "The Prison Community", published in 1940, found that many prison inmates were unattached or "ungrouped." This occurred in part in response to the official injunction to inmates to "do your own time", that is stay away from close and intimate association with other prisoners. Inmates have been compensated for being what has been called "social isolates", by such meaningful rewards as time credits toward earlier parole. In the revised edition of Clemmer's book, Donald R. Cressey* has pointed out interestingly that this emphasis upon psychological isolation has replaced an earlier one upon physical isolation** as a means of social control. When effectively conducted, group counse-

---

*   Clemmer, D., "The Prison Community, New York, Holt, 1958, page IX.

**   Physical isolation is illustrated by the Pennsylvania plan for the separate confinement of prisoners. Barnes, H.E., and Teeters, N.K., in the third revised edition of their text, "New Horizons in Criminology", Englewood Cliffs, N.J., Prentice-Hall, 1959, have described on page 339 the operation of the penitentiary in Philadelphia known as "Cherry Hill". The prisoner "worked, ate, slept in his cell and saw no one but the officers of the institution, and official visitors from the outside community."

ling seems to bring about changes in some of the psychological characteristics of the prison community, especially in the so-called "inmate culture" described by Clemmer and others. One has necessarily to spend some time in an institution wherein a majority of the staff and inmates are genuinely responsive to group counseling to appreciate these changes. Major research studies now being carried out may soon contribute more objective answers to these and other claims for group counseling.

In this connection, group counseling may provide, as Harrison has pointed out, an antidote "to the negative form of inmate led and criminally oriented group counseling that has been going on in prisons and jails since they first started and which has tended to make them schools of crime."[*] Korn and McCorkle[**] have used the concept of resocialization in discussing this possible outcome of treatment in prison. They expressed this succintly as follows:

> "As the concept "socialization" implies group membership, so the derivative concept "resocialization" implies changes in group memberships. Many findings in the social origins of individual behavior suggest that the problems of reshaping the antisocial values and attitudes of offenders is related to the possibility of altering the patterns of group membership which they bring with them into the prison."

The second requirement, if group counseling is

---

[*]   Harrison, R.M., "Mental Health Applications in the California Correctional System, The Chatham Conference, Boston University, 1960, page 62.

[**] Korn, R.R., and McCorkle, L.W., "Criminology and Penology", New York, Holt, 1959, page 551.

to be carried on effectively, is <u>a condition of</u>
<u>mutual acceptance among those in the group.</u> In other
words, not only must the group feel free to discuss
their problems, as just mentioned, but the general
atmosphere in which they do so must be supportive.
That is, there must be reasonably good human relationships among members of the group and between
the group leader and the inmates or clients. When
human beings genuinely accept each other as persons,
they are better able to help each other with their
problems. This is especially true in the treatment
of those in conflict with the law, because rejection,
the poisonous opposite of acceptance, so often seems
to have played a significant role in the explanation
of the origin of the symptoms of criminality.

It is believed that in the early life of the
criminal, rejective treatment by other people, notably parents or others in authority, has been a
significant factor in arousing and establishing
feelings of hostility or resentment. These are believed to have subsequently a causal relationship
to stealing or robbery or assaultive behavior. The
evidence of helpfulness and good will toward the
inmate, the opposite of rejection, which the employee
and the other inmates show in group counseling, are
important constructive factors in whatever effectiveness the program may have.

The essence of helpfulness in a relationship
originates in the mutually trustful understanding
between the group leader and the client and in their
liking and respect for each other. This thesis has
been abundantly documented by citations of research
studies in a recent article by Rogers,* a leader in
the scientific study of counseling. In general, the

---

*   Rogers, C.R., "The Characteristics of a Helping
Relationship", The Personnel and Guidance Journal, 1958 XXXVII,. 6-16.

procedures and techniques used, he has stated, are secondary to the warm and accepting attitudes, and the freedom of the client to make choices and to respond spontaneously in the treatment situation.

When group counseling is conducted adequately, there is among those present the comfortable feeling of being in the company of sympathetic persons, the leader and the group. This good emotional climate in the group is one of the basic requirements for any accomplishment by way of treatment. If the client's efforts to face his problems meet with interest and respect, his future welfare and the best interests of society may both be served. The client's acceptance by the group as a person who needs and seeks help may be an initial step in his course toward rehabilitation. This acceptance does not imply exoneration. In the group discussions, the behavior of the offender is not condoned. Although there is warm and sympathetic acceptance of his desire to change, his offense is not excused nor are the victims and the injuries suffered by them disregarded or forgotten.

How and why the group, in which there is mutual acceptance, may be helpful has been clearly stated by the eminent psychiatrist, Doctor William C. Menninger, in the following quotation from a publication of the National Association for Mental Health:

"If we become aware of problems in ourselves or if we want to be of help to a member of the family or a friend, we have to know something about emotional first aid. Many times one can get help by merely talking over the problem with a trusted friend, a member of the family, a teacher, minister, or sometimes a co-worker. Just being able to talk about the problem to someone who will listen sympathetically and perhaps throw a new light on it may go far towards its solution."

50

THE MAJOR OBJECTIVES OF GROUP COUNSELING:

When these two fundamental requirements have been met, the goals of group counseling may be pursued successfully. The first of these is to help prisoners adjust to the frustrations which are an unalterable part of life in an institution and in society. Inmates may find relief in noting in other members of the group the same disturbances of feelings which they themselves have. If there is good movement in the group, that is, active interest and effort, counselees may also profit from seeing how others strive to face and to deal with their problems. In some instances, the feelings expressed by others in the group may arouse an awareness in the listeners of similar, but hitherto unrecognized, feelings in themselves.

When effective, group counseling may lead to better adjustment to the frustrations encountered in the jail or prison or under supervision in society. Topics discussed by the group in a correctional institution include the conditions of institutional living and the reasons for various rules and regulations imposed by the institutional authorities. These group discussions may at times be relatively calm and patient or they may sometimes include expressions of strong hostile feelings about the conditions of life in the institution or elsewhere.

As they grow in maturity through these frank discussions, inmates begin to understand better the need for the tolerance of the certain-to-be frustrations of jail or prison life. They may note the relationships of these institutional sources of annoyance or resentment to the equally certain-to-occur unpleasant circumstances after release from detention when a similar need for self control will face them.

As for the seemingly unnecessary frustrations

in institutional life, inmates are permitted to tell about their grievances or to express hostilities with diminishing fear or anxiety as they become more secure in the presence of the accepting, non-punishing group leader. Those who do not talk, may also profit from the effects upon them of being present while other inmates in the group are permitted to express their hostilities. Sometimes, surprisingly, the more silent members of the group seem to profit from what goes on in group counseling as much or even more than those who talk the most. It is important for the reader to note that the group leader's permissiveness toward inmate expressions of hostility toward him or toward the administration of the institution or toward authority elsewhere may serve as a model of permissiveness for the inmates when they begin their own criticism of each other.

After the clients gain security in the group counseling situation, they can more readily discuss the frustrations of jail or prison or of life under supervision in the community. Under the best circumstances, they begin to realize how many restrictions of freedom are necessary in the conduct of an institution or an agency. They may also grow to accept their own responsibility for the fact that they are now in a position where they must be subjected to frustrating conditions.

Men in jail or prison sometimes imagine the world outside to be a paradise compared with the institution. To parolees or probationers, as to others in society, the frustrations in daily living in society are known to be quite numerous. The need of the probationer or parolee is to face the unalterable frustrations in life itself and to achieve the maturity to accept them with reasonable fortitude. Especially does he need to realize that unless he does so, only trouble will occur for himself and for others who are dependent upon him. The man in the institution, like the probationer or parolee, needs to realize that society contains inevitable frustrations, to which he must learn to adjust more maturely if he is to remain out of trouble. A more understanding acceptance of reality is a major objective of group counseling.

A second goal of group counseling in correctional practice is to enable the clients to recognize the significance of emotional conflicts as underlying criminality. A prisoner, previously unaware of the emotional basis of his crimes, or unwilling even to recognize feelings as part of their causation, may be helped to achieve a better understanding of himself by what is said by others in the group. The client may also appreciate the significance of resentful feelings toward authority figures, such as parents, employers, or law enforcement officials as suggesting possibly a partial explanation of why he has been in trouble.

The examination of his own emotional disturbances and hearing about those of others in the group, and the experience of relating these feelings to criminal behavior may lead to better understanding of how such behavior originates. The client has to accept himself as someone with costly disturbances of feeling, costly in that they have brought him loss of freedom and many other troubles and tragedies. After weeks of group counseling, he should gradually become secure enough in the group to be at least open-minded regarding the above belief that the release and examination of his inner feelings in the group and frankness in telling about them, are likely to be helpful for his future well being and happiness in society. This is more advantageous than folding his arms and merely stating that he is in trouble because of being lazy or from lack of will power.

A third objective of group counseling is the opportunity for the client to learn from his peers about the social aspects of his personality, that is, how he affects others, as he associates with those about him. He can learn the effects of his personality upon others in the permissive setting of group counseling. He is told frankly about both his shortcomings and his good traits by his fellow inmates. To be told the same things, for example, that he seems willing to go to any lengths, even to criminality, to impress others, to be told this by those in authority may be less effective, because probably other authority figures have failed previously in his life in trying to help him to recognize and overcome this fault.

A fourth goal of group counseling is the advancement of self-study in the group, which makes possible a better understanding of the world of make-believe, of phantasy, and how costly may be behavioral responses to the antisocial content of day-dreams. Any disturbed, unhappy individual may find some elements of relief in day-dreaming. The probationer's or inmate's day-dreaming* may be especially absorbing. It becomes costly to him if it leads to criminal behavior and to jail or prison.

The importance of control of socially undesirable actions arising from day-dreaming - that is, day-dreaming which issues from unhappy or otherwise disturbed feelings - is discussed in Chapter I of the textbook prepared for inmates of correctional institutions, entitled, "What Will Be Your Life?** To recognize the undesirable behavioral outcomes

---

*   Healy, W., and Bronner, A., have described this psychological process in "Delinquents and Criminals, Their Making and Unmaking", New York, Macmillan, 1926, 317 pp, and in "New Lights on Delinquency and its Treatment", New Haven, Yale University Press, 1938, 226 pp.

** Released by the American Correctional Association, 135 East 15th St., New York, 3, N.Y., 1957, 108 pp.

of day-dreaming about alleged injustices or perse-
cutions toward himself, phantasies of revenge, of
self-vindication or making up to himself for his
sufferings, or of actual criminal deeds is one of
the major problems which face inmates of the jail
or prison who want "to get out and stay out", and
parolees and probationers, who want to be discharged
from supervision and to remain in society. The lack
of control over the anti-social actions associated
with or resulting from day-dreaming is what is costly in the life of the offender.

Finally, a fifth objective of group counseling
is the improvement of the emotional climate of the
institution. Group counseling and other methods of
treatment may contribute to the transformation of
the jail or the prison or other correctional agency,
so that it comes nearer to being a place where people may reasonably or justifiably expect to receive
helpful treatment. The training and treatment program in the jail, farm unit, honor camp or prison,
to be most effective, must find support in the acceptance of treatment by the entire staff. There
should be a sympathetic desire on the part of all
personnel to help the inmates in their efforts at
self-understanding and self-control. The same team
work should be encountered by clients on parole or
probation or those referred to a social agency.
Group counseling has been of value in bringing nearer the important goal of genuine team work in the
agency.

The most advanced correctional institutions
and agencies of today are places where every reasonable consideration is given to the clients as
human beings with troubles. The treatment resources
of education, vocational training, religion, medi-
cine, work, recreation, psychology, psychiatry,
social work, and other disciplines are utilized as
fully as staff and other resources and architectural
conditions permit. Group counseling may advance the
program of the above areas of treatment in the good

institution or agency by its recognition of the needs for growth in the personality development of the inmates. It utilizes the values of constructive group dynamics, the psychological interaction of people in a group, in trying to meet these needs.

The mutual acceptance of clients and employees in the good and considerate agency or institution of today may be implemented by group counseling to help to transform these places so that the inmates realize that something is being attempted in order to rehabilitate them. Only as those primarily concerned with the custodial program and as employees in the different phases of treatment join together in a mutually cooperative program, can the correctional institution become a place for treatment. Likewise, in the parole or probation office, all directly concerned with clients as well as those indirectly involved through staff supervision, must convince others of their sincere belief in the viewpoint of treatment.

The overall atmosphere of a social agency, like a welfare department or a probation or parole office, is more difficult to evaluate. Unlike an institution where the inmates are in residence, the probation office is merely a central clearing house for the staff, whose activities are widely scattered in the community. Yet even under these circumstances, in the parole or probation office the spirit of the place, the attitudes of the staff as a whole, whether they are predominantly punitive or predominantly therapeutic, have a broad influence upon what can be done for the clients. A major objective of group counseling is to enable the caseworkers in these places to do what most of them sincerely want to do, namely to gain better rapport and to relate and work more constructively with their clients.

INDIVIDUAL COUNSELING RELATED TO THE GROUP PROGRAM:

A valuable by-product or accompaniment of group counseling may be noted in the assistance rendered by the group leader incidentally in the form of individual counseling. The client may approach the group leader before or after the session and ask for advice or guidance with some personal problems. At such times group leaders may be helpful to their counselees in many details of living through such informal individual conferences. It is an accepted part of the group counseling program that when clients come to group leaders with practical problems, they may, if their knowledge permits, answer their questions. If unable to do so with confidence, then they should know enough about institutional or agency operations to direct the client to the individual on the staff most likely to be helpful and even to try to make an appointment for the counselee to confer with him.

Future studies may indicate that probation officers or parole agents may find group counseling of practical value in the more economical handling of their caseloads. Ordinarily, it would seem advisable that they should serve both as the group leaders and as the individual caseworkers for the clients in their group. With a large caseload, group counseling may possibly be a helpful device for assuring that the parole agent or probation officer will be in touch with his clients more often than is possible when visits have to be made to individual residences, or with less effort than when arrangements have to be made for individual appointments in the office.

SOME GENERAL VALUES OF GROUP COUNSELING:

As a reflection perhaps of the accomplishment of the just cited required conditions and objectives of group counseling, there are other goals of a more general character. The first of these is <u>the help</u>

given clients in facing and realizing some of the
duties and obligations of life in a democracy. A
study of the group counseling program at the California State Prison at Folsom made by Julius Samuel*
in the early days of the program there noted a number of values. One of those cited was a gain in the
understanding of ethical and social principles.
These Samuels included with others under the heading
of informal educational values. The group discussions
led prisoners to a greater knowledge of the conditions of their lives as persons. They discussed
questions about any aspects of prison life that were
of concern to them.

These discussions lead naturally to the meaning
of social life elsewhere in society. In them, clients
may analyse, as did the naval personnel reported in
an earlier chapter, the privileges of persons living
in American communities and also the related obligations to their country. These discussions of social
ethics in turn lead to the study of the meaning of
socially acceptable experience; in other words, of
participation in activities in society, which are
for the general welfare. Inmates in a well conducted counseling group discuss aspects of their lives
from moral or ethical standpoints which would be
taboo in the ordinary prison yard. These include
the admission of feelings of good will toward others.
It has been noted in work with offenders how difficult it is for them to express tender feelings in
the group.

Another impressive educational outcome of group
counseling is a notable improvement among the clients
in speaking before others. In some cases, this may
be of considerable value for personality development.

---

* Presented in "A Review of Present Problems in
the Group Counseling Program", Represa, California, July, 1956, 8 pages, mimeographed.

58

The advancement of socially desirable activities during leisure time is another value mentioned by Samuels in his study of the group counseling program. The use of arts and crafts in group treatment has long been a practice of Slavson and others in their work with younger subjects.* It has not been developed as yet in the adult program in the prisons.

Concern with correctional objectives should not blind us to the recognition of recreational values in group counseling. This is not the primary goal of the program, but, as Samuels noted, group counseling brings gratification and relaxation to the members of the group. These pleasant and wholesome feelings are valuable outcomes of group counseling.

SOME VALUES FOR EMPLOYEES:

At various places throughout this volume mention is made of job satisfactions to the staff from participation in group counseling, or even from working in an institution or agency wherein group counseling is part of the treatment program. Thus, group leaders have reported being rewarded by observations of the growth toward maturity of individual members of their groups. Vocational instructors and tradesmen who have conducted groups in their own shops have observed more interest and alertness in the inmates and greater friendliness toward themselves. They have seen evidences of improvement in mutual good will among the inmates. Not only did they believe that the general morale of the shops improved, but in addition they reported an increase in productive output.

Formerly many good employees left prison work because of the painful boredom of merely guarding people for long hours each week. Participation in

---

*   See Slavson, S.R., "An Introduction to Group Therapy", New York, The Commonwealth Fund, 1950, 352 pp.

group counseling has resulted in giving more interest and meaning to their work with inmates. Warden Fred R. Dickson of San Quentin, who has had a long and distinguished career in penology, has stated the opinion that promising correctional officers are more likely to continue in the prison service because of the greater feelings of accomplishment they experience as group leaders.

SUMMARY OF THE CHAPTER:

Some of the conditions prerequisite to the effective conduct of group counseling and the objectives sought have been discussed in this chapter. When these are achieved, one of the impressive effects noted has been the better morale of the agency or the institution. The improvement in the emotional climate of the place would be fostered by the more wholesome and hopeful feelings the clients have about themselves, and the increased good will among them toward each other and toward the staff. Objective evidence of these advances in the institution has been a decrease in serious disciplinary incidents after the introduction of group counseling as the inmate-staff communication improves.

With the parolee or probationer, similar results may be expected; that is, better attitudes toward the acceptance of the necessary regulations that are imposed and a greater willingness to discuss their problems frankly with their probation officers or parole agents. It is believed that these clients may show a decrease in fear, suspicion or distrust of those in authority. The morale of the group leader and the clients and their relationships to each other improve as the counseling group matures. The participants become part of the same team, whose goal is the social well being and adjustment of the clients. The constructive purposes of correctional casework, we believe, have a greater chance to approach reality in an agency wherein adequately conducted group counseling has been achieved.

CHAPTER 5

TREATMENT IN CORRECTIONAL AND AGENCIES

PROGRESS TOWARD TREATMENT IN CORRECTIONAL WORK:

It cannot be mentioned too often or emphasized too much, that practically all inmates of jail and prisons return sooner or later to society. Experience suggests that brutality toward them in prison, or even humane but impersonal handling is unlikely to make them good neighbors when they return to the community. The treatment institution, on the contrary, offers much better insurance for the inmate's future welfare and for the best interests of society, since inmates therein, through training and treatment and through individual or group counseling or psychotherapy, may learn how to adjust to their needs and gain in self-control.

If prisons, jails, honor camps, and other detention facilities are to be of better recognized service to society, to be more than merely humane places to which socially maladjusted persons may be temporarily banished, they must become institutions which resemble the general hospital in that their diagnostic and treatment functions are clearly defined. Likewise, probation and parole must develop methods of dealing with persons who have been previously errant in society in such a way that all concerned, officers and clients, work together within a program designed not merely for control through supervision, but more especially for helpful guidance and treatment for the purpose of rehabilitation.

Institutions for the physically ill have advanced to the modern hospital from places which people dreaded to enter. In earlier times, patients

enter a hospital for one illness and if they
,ived that, might die of another caught there be-
.use of lack of hygienic precautions. Consequently,
the forerunners of the modern hospital became in the
minds of ordinary people places of danger and ill
repute.

To bring about a change from this dreadful
situation, several notable developments took place
in hospital administration. In the first place,
diagnostic methods were improved. On this basis,
the hospital staff was able to learn more adequately what was wrong with the patients. They were able
to classify them. As additional wards were made
available, hospitals began to segretate those suffering from one kind of contagious disease from
those afflicted with others. Patients were placed
in wards especially designed for their needs in matters of observation and care.

More recently, hospital staffs and administrators tried successfully to make the hospital more
pleasant and cheerful for the patients. Not only
were physical hygiene and sanitation improved, but
hospitals became more attractive places as the de-
corations and furnishings of the rooms and wards
were selected with an eye to cheerful and harmonious
colors. Coincident with these improvements came better resources for training hospital personnel. Morale improved. The good will and optimism of doctors
and nurses were recognized as important in treatment.

With improvements in diagnosis and the recognition of the causes of physical diseases came ad-
vancements in methods of treatment. All cases were
not treated similarly. Each kind of disease came
gradually to be treated differently from all others.
As the diagnosis and treatment improved, and the
staffs of doctors and nurses recognized these advances, the morale of the hospital grew better.
People in general were more willing to accept the

hospital as a place to go for treatment.*

Similar advances have also occurred more recently in mental hospitals. An illustration of the impressive changes that took place in the staff of a
custodial type of mental hospital may be of interest.
Some widely heralded treatment facilities were introduced there. Patients were treated who had been
considered hopeless for rehabilitation. Previously
these patients had been housed and cared for humane-
ly, but now for the first time they received treatment that seemed likely to help them to advance mentally, and even possibly to leave the hospital and
return to society. The constructive effects upon morale of the staff were, as the superintendent re-
marked, "electric." The patients also became more
responsive as they saw these new developments and
responded to the more optimistic attitudes and feelings of the staff.

Many correctional facilities and agencies are
undergoing similar changes.** Among many other advances, one that is especially significant is that
employees of the jail or the prison, like those in
a good hospital, have begun to understand and respect the rehabilitative purposes of their institutions. They are interested in and collaborate
hopefully in programs of treatment. Workers in the
jail, honor camp, or prison, like the employees of

---

* See, however, Saunders, L., "Cultural Difference
  and Medical Care", New York, N.Y., Russell Sage
  Foundation, 1954, 317 pp., for an interesting
  account of current fears and superstition about
  clinics and hospitals.

** Some of the new programs and administrative innovations that have lead toward this treatment
  viewpoint in the prisons of California, are discussed in: Fenton, N., "The Prisoner's Family",
  Palo Alto, California, Pacific Books, 1959, p.6-9.

a good hospital, now enjoy greater self-respect and more genuine interest and even enthusiasm in their work. At the same time the general public has become more appreciative of services rendered by these institutions.

The advancement in the public appreciation of the probation officer and his program of treatment has also been notable. The recognition of the social contributions of parole agents, though slower in developing, has begun to advance as the public becomes better informed of their constructive activities on behalf of parolees and their important role in society.

In this volume, we are concerned with some theoretical and practical considerations about group counseling and its constructive influences upon the jail, the prison, parole, and probation. With few exceptions, correctional institutions were relatively humane, but until recently, like the hospitals of earlier times, not impressive to the objective observer as places for treatment. A fundamental outcome of some recently added programs, including group counseling, has been to further desired changes toward the acceptance of treatment in the correctional institution.

The basic treatment objective, the return of the inmates to society better prepared than when admitted to adjust there, becomes more widely accepted as the principal purpose of correctional institutions in the minds of both staff members and inmates. Group counseling has helped in the prisons to bring about an institutional climate where there is more courteous, mutually respectful, and friendly communication among the staff members themselves, among the inmate group, and between employees and inmates.

These desirable attitudes seem also to lead to the considerate treatment of the relatives and friends of inmates who visit the treatment institution. This

is done not only because the relatives are accepted
as deserving courteous consideration as persons,
but also because of the recognition of the potential
values of family and friends in plans for the rehabilitation of inmates. Likewise, the inclusion of
relatives and others in the community in the correctional program is becoming more evident in the
work of probation and parole departments.

TREATMENT THROUGH CONSTRUCTIVE HUMAN RELATIONSHIPS:

At various places reference is made to the
major hypothesis of this volume, that treatment
through constructive human relationships, characterized primarily by the mutual acceptance of the
group leader and his counselees, may lead to greater
maturity in clients. The opposite kinds of human
relationships, destructive or rejective ones, have
also been presented as likely to create greater im-
maturity, and consequently to increase the serious-
ness of the anti-social behavior of institutioal-
ized offenders before and after release.

What is meant by these two forces, may be somewhat clarified by the analysis offered in Chart I.
The method of presentation used therein illustrates
the extremes of traits of personality noted by the
writer over the years in his work with prison employees and others in the field of correctional
work. These traits have been observed to be associated on the one hand with those inclined to give
inmates or other clients impersonal and severe custodial care and supervision, and on the other with
those concerned with them as human beings and sup-
porting a program of treatment. It should be noted
also that some "practical" penologists in good faith
still believe that severity of regulations, maintained with an iron hand and even perhaps associated
with physical punishment, lead more effectively
than does treatment to the prevention of institu-

65

tional disorders and recidivism. From our viewpoint, we may recall in this connection a quotation attributed to Samuel Johnson, "Severity is a way to govern, not to mend."

The presentation of contrasting viewpoints in Chart I has been generalized for emphasis. Few, if any, conscientious, custodially minded persons are at the extreme of the traits listed for them. Only a minority of treatment-minded employees ever achieve the ideals presented in Chart I on their side of the picture. Chart I may be justifiably criticized as subjective. It needs to be tested by the tabulation of better controlled observations.

CHART I

VIEWPOINTS IN INSTITUTIONAL PRACTICE

THE EMPLOYEE WITH A CONSTRUCTIVE INFLUENCE	THE EMPLOYEE WITH A DESTRUCTIVE INFLUENCE
Studies causation: Why does the inmate behave as he does?	Concentrates attention upon outward behavior.
Is tolerant.	May be suspicious or even prejudiced.
Is patient.	May be irritable.
Is thoughtful and considerate.	Habitually impersonal.
Requests explanations of errors or misbehavior.	May report inmates in a severe manner without asking them for an explanation.
Is persuasive.	Is authoritarian.

66

Correctional workers who proceed according to the viewpoints of treatment in Chart I have at the outset encountered difficulties. For one thing, they have been insecure themselves, in part unconsciously, or because of concern over the opposition of some of their colleagues who prefer the older punishment beliefs and practices. The newer treatment methods have often been ridiculed by opponents; one common exaggerative figure of speech is that they transform the prison into a country club. Even in an institution where in-service training had been carried on for a number of years, the first employees who participated in group counseling were subjected to severely critical comments from their colleagues.

In view of our present knowledge of penology we believe that a strictly authoritarian, severely punitive prison, as the recent riots have demonstrated, seems not to be the answer for the sincere penologist. Although riots activated by psychopathic inmates may occur in any correctional institution, the overwhelming number of prison riots have taken place in prisons that were inhumane, punitive and largely custodial in orientation. Observations of inmates in the punitive, custodially-oriented prison suggest that prisoners therein have confirmed feelings that all authority is harsh and to be distrusted. They show their attitudes toward authority by many forms of overt and covert hostility to the correctional staff. These include catcalls, booing, obscene sounds, sarcastic comments loud enough to be heard, contemptuous looks, an overall hard, cold indifference. This behavior is well illustrated by what has been called figuratively, "the dog-eye", a thoroughly insulting unspoken inmate reaction. The culminating forms of inmate hostility include insults, physical attacks and finally riots. For their part, many officers in these places are observed to have some of the qualities listed in Chart I under the custodial viewpoint.

It is not surprising that sociologists studying

the punitive, custodially-oriented institutions
arrive at the concept of two separate cultures in
the prison, one the inmate culture and the other
that of the staff. Nor is it surprising that they
find the objectives of these two cultures in conflict with each other. This sociological hypothesis,
possibly accurate enough for the ordinary "tough"
prison, needs to be modified if applied in correctional institutions wherein treatment is accorded
a genuinely high status. In the latter places, the
inmates seem to be more accepting of the officers.
The evidences of hostility mentioned above occur
rarely. There may, however, still be symptomatic
evidences of individual personality disturbances.
One must expect some mental aberration in any large
prison population.

Expressions of an antagonistic inmate rejection
of the staff, the evidence for the alleged inmate
culture, are not so prominent in the treatment institution. Group counseling, some believe, may prove
to be one of the innovations which may contribute
considerably to growth toward the greater integra-
tion of the purposes of the inmates and the staff
in the treatment institution. Current studies seem
to indicate the value of group counseling in bringing
about more wholesome communication between prison
inmates and the staff of the correctional institution.
Major research investigations now in progress may
soon contribute significant findings as to the accu-
racy of these predictions concerning future developments in correctional treatment.

PROGRESS TOWARD "SERVICE" IN THE SOCIAL AGENCY:

Recently an interesting document was prepared by
social scientists entitled, "The Road Ahead for
California's Needy Children."* It contains a stimu-

---

* Prepared by a Task Force under the leadership
of Arthur W. Potts, and released by the State
Department of Social Welfare, Sacramento,
California, 1960, 64 pages.

lating analysis of this important and extensive welfare program. In reading it, one may recognize that the welfare department, like any organization caring for people, has many required and necessary procedures or controls. In a public welfare organization these include the determination of eligibility for aid, the correctness of the assigned grant and other administrative matters.

With the burdens of heavy caseloads, it is not surprising that some local welfare agencies have, to quote the report*, "assumed that their major role was to pass on the eligibility of persons requesting aid and to assure that those eligible received the proper grants. <u>Service has too often been viewed as an "extra" to be provided when possible, but not a consistent focus.</u>" (The italics are ours.) Presumably, "service" in welfare agencies is a term similar in its implication to "treatment" in correctional work. "Service" includes the means which the agency uses to help the individual attain his highest potentiality.

It seems inevitable that there be competition for staff attention in the welfare agency between the important details concerned with administrative procedures and the measures involved in providing service or treatment. In view of the sizes of caseloads and other factors, the worker may have little or no time to offer any service to clients. Obviously, when assigned a heavy caseload, the correctional employee and the social worker may be alike in being prevented through insufficient time from giving much attention to "service" or "treatment." The report commendably recommends that "the purpose of the ANC program be restated to provide a clear direction for the development of a program of dependency preventation, protection of children, rehabilitation and financial maintenance to all needy families with children."**

---

*   Ibid, page 49.

** Ibid, page 49.

In the prisons, an economical transition toward treatment, while continuing to maintain security, was facilitated by many devices, among them, group counseling conducted by other than professional clinicians. Its use came about in part as a compromise between the need for an army of clinicians to conduct group psychotherapy (impossible of achieving as a budgetary reality) or doing nothing "extra"; that is, adding to the training program of most inmates little or nothing which would be specifically directed toward their personality adjustment. The group counseling program proved to be a fortunate development in the move toward treatment. Not only in the California prisons, but more recently in correctional institutions and agencies elsewhere, group counseling has been introduced as an economical and effective means of advancing the program of correctional treatment.

GROUP TREATMENT IN THE SOCIAL WELFARE PROGRAM:

In reading "The Road Ahead for California's Needy Children" one question raised is, What, if any, "service" can be provided to welfare recipients within a budgetary reality? And this leads naturally to the question raised in this volume and focussed upon at this point, What practical usefulness may group counseling have if used by case workers in the welfare programs?

Probably some may object to bringing. together. welfare recipients in groups, as was true when prison inmates and especially parolees were first handled in groups. Conscientious parole officers had rather serious anxieties several years ago when for the first time a group of parolees were brought together at night in the San Francisco Office of the Division of Adult Parolees. Their fears proved to be unfounded. The men arrived rather promptly and responded well at the meeting. As the evening progressed, and over the coffee cups toward its end, good feelings increased in the group. A number of values were noted;

parolees were of help to each other, for example, by suggesting job opportunities for the few who were unemployed or not satisfied with their jobs. After the meeting, the parolees went to their places of residence much in the manner in which lodge members disperse and go home. The terrible crime wave that some of the more anxious individuals anticipated, did not occur. This experience is further evidence of how much time and attention we give to worrying about things that never happen! Moreover, we may repeat the question once raised by Richard A. McGee before a group of overly fearful prison administrators, "How is progress to occur in enterprises for human welfare, unless in trying something new we are prepared to take some calculated risks?"

On the positive side, we may ask, if groups of welfare recipients were to meet together, is it not likely that they, too, like the parolees, would have helpful and positive suggestions for each other? Actually, Wiltse and Fixl* who conducted a program of group work in the welfare department in San Francisco were emphatic in their statement, "our project experience convinced us that the use of groups should complement the traditional individual approaches in all phases of the public assistance agency's work with its clients." Their conclusions supported the belief that the use of the group process would be an important factor in counteracting unfortunate psychological reactions in welfare recipients, such as feelings of inadequacy, inferiority or hopelessness. They found the group process helpful in a variety of other ways, including the determination of eligibility, mutual assistance of clients with personal problems, suggestions from the group for economical and tasteful

*   Wiltse, K.T., and Fixl, J., "A Study of the Administration of the ADC Program", published in ADC: Problem and Promise, Chicago, Illinois, American Public Welfare Association, 1960, page 30.

menus, places to shop most advantageously, and advice regarding job finding. The group could also provide each other with supportive help in profiting from the use of public clinics and other health resources available for welfare recipients. Other minor practical outcomes might possibly be cooperation in baby sitting or even advice regarding reasonable places to live. Unfortunately, however, although Wiltse and Fixl saw some possible use of group methods by workers in welfare agencies who are not fully trained in social psychiatry, they did not specify in detail the types of clients or problems such persons might be encouraged to approach with group methods.

If group counseling were tried with welfare clients, constructive group interaction might also occur, as it occurred in the group meetings of the prospective mothers in the pre-natal clinic mentioned earlier. Just as group counseling did much for the morale of these prospective mothers, so also would one be justified in expecting a similar advance in the constructive feelings and attitudes of recipients of aid in the social agency. In some cases, the mere fact of being on public assistance may cause an immediate trend toward personality disintegration similar in effect to what happens to some offenders after being placed in custody.

Even a very slight personal recognition may have a counteractive effect to these distressing trends. Group counseling is one method by which the individual is recognized as a person, finds help in the understanding and good will of others, especially the group leader, and may overcome the tendencies toward hopelessness and despair. The absence of treatment for these negative attitudes and behavior in those receiving public assistance is contrary to the legislative intent as quoted in "The Road Ahead for California's Needy Children." This intent was spelled out in the law as shown in the following quotation: "That assistance shall be so administered as to encourage self-respect, self-reliance, and the desire to be a good citizen, useful to society."*

The experiences in the use of group treatment with welfare clients described by Louise P. Shoemaker are illuminating and inspiring. From her work in Baltimore, she concluded** that "the experiences of the groups of mothers receiving assistance through ADC confirmed the agency's fears about some of the deep seated anxiety, mistrust and resentment of clients toward social workers and agency. These experiences have revealed some of the problems of living on assistance, of fatherless homes and husbandless women, and of community attitudes toward public assistance recipients. But I feel the deeper purpose has also been served; that some of the clients who have been involved in this new service have recognized these problems in their lives, have expressed their feelings about them, and through the group experience, which was focused on the meaning to them of being recipients of public assistance, have begun to take hold of doing something toward a better life for themselves and their children."

OBSTACLES TO GROUP COUNSELING IN WELFARE AGENCIES:

Some doubts about the introduction of group counseling in the welfare agency will undoubtedly be raised, as is usually the case when change is proposed. Among the practical concerns would be many of the same obstacles found in correctional agencies, such as limitations of staff, the lack of adequate places for groups to meet, insufficient resources for the supervision of the program, and the absence of other necessities for its desirable

---

* Ibid, page 8.

** Shoemaker, L.P., "The Use of the Social Group Work Method in Offering a More Comprehensive Service to Mothers Receiving ADC", Journal of Social Work Process, 1960, XI, page 105.

operation. A serious question has been raised whether there might be some violations of confidentiality; whether, for example, some clients might be hurt because persons in the group or because neighbors might learn somehow that they were on public assistance. Lack of resources to provide additional in-service training for the workers involved in group counseling may be another serious obstacle. In order to introduce and develop the program, special staff preparation and training are necessary on a continuing basis. This may not be possible if the caseloads are too large and other demands upon workers and supervisors are also excessive.

Another major obstacle may be a psychological one, growing out of the anxieties or threats to workers involved in the change of their activities from a one-to-one relationship with clients to use of the group as a means of treatment. This change may threaten the caseworker's own security, especially if he has long been accustomed to individualized methods of dealing with clients. For this reason, the use of group counseling should be limited at first to those workers and clients who are interested in trying it. It would be undesirable to use any compulsion in its introduction or to imply that it is the only method to use or even a necessary one.

Preliminary explorations in a number of county welfare departments in California and in similar agencies in other states have shown that a variety of gains can be achieved by the use of group methods. We have noted that after its application in correctional institutions, improvements occurred in the attitudes of employees toward their work and especially in their greater acceptance of the viewpoint of treatment. If group counseling should prove feasible and practical and could be introduced into social agencies with arrangement to adjust the program to meet the obstacles just recited, it would be reasonable to expect a similar good effect upon the morale of the staff.

SUMMARY: THE GROUP SUPPORT OF GOOD INTENTIONS:

Group counseling may have the advantage of enabling us to reach and to treat the personality problems of clients more economically and effectively than by individual counseling. Moreover, experience suggests that by virtue of constructive interaction in the group, members may help each other. The expression of feelings by one client may be influential in enabling some of the others in the group to recognize and deal with similar feelings in themselves. They may communicate with each other not only intellectually, but also on what might be called a feeling level. The reader may confirm from his own experience, that words may often not be adequate to describe one's feelings. The interplay of feelings in the group, whether or not expressed in words, helps the attentive inmates to dissolve some defenses or resistances interfering with their own release of feelings. Moreno, a pioneer in group psychotherapy, has epitomized the significance of this interaction in the statement, "The locus of the therapeutic influence is in the group rather than in the therapist."*

The expressed wishes and good intentions of an inmate to leave and not return to jail or prison, or the desire of a client to complete probation, or to be off the welfare rolls, may strengthen members of the listening group who have similar problems to accept their own inner or deeper feelings of wanting to adjust better in society. Carl R. Rogers**, who has made important contributions to counseling, has expressed with some conviction the belief that human

---

* Moreno, J.L., "The First Book on Group Psychotherapy", New York, Beacon House, 1957, page XI.

** Rogers, C.R., in Mowrer's "Psychotherapy", New York, Ronald Press, 1953, 700 pp.

nature is basically wholesome. In most people, according to this hypothesis, the desire exists to conform, to be accepted by others, and to get along well in society. However, not all philosophers or social scientists, it should be noted, are in agreement regarding this optimistic viewpoint.

Group counseling may be considered a medium in which jail or prison inmates or clients in community agencies may examine the conditions of their lives. On their own initiative they may strive to recognize the costs of what they have done to themselves and to others, including their own families and the victims of their misdeeds. Many of them may seek earnestly to unearth the origins of their own tendencies toward undesirable behaviors and the means to overcome them.

One of the basic problems in the personality development of clients is how they may develop good feelings and attitudes, how they may grow in self-esteem. After gaining some hopeful feelings about themselves, they may be encouraged to establish their own native good will toward others as a directive in control of their lives. This hope can be fostered in an environment where others are also struggling to do likewise.

The following rather figurative quotation from Roger's article*, in which he expresses the above viewpoint, is appropriate as the ending of this chapter:

––––––––––––

* Rogers, C.R., in Mowrer's "Psychotherapy", New York, Ronald Press, 1953, Chapter II, page 67.

"When man is less than fully man, when
he denies to awareness various aspects of
his experience, then indeed we have all too
often reason to fear him and his behavior,
as the present world situation testifies.
But when he is more fully man, when he is
his complete organism, when awareness of
experience, a peculiarly human attribute,
is most fully operating, then he is to be
trusted, then his behavior is constructive.
It is not always conventional. It will not
always be conforming. It will be individualized, but it will also be socialized."

CHAPTER 6

ADMINISTRATIVE CONSIDERATIONS IN THE GROUP COUNSELING PROGRAM

GROUP COUNSELING AND INSTITUTIONAL SECURITY:

Group counseling, in the experience of the prisons of California, has been advantageous not only in enhancing treatment but also for improving security. For example, a statistical analysis of escapes showed proportionately fewer among counselees than among a comparable group not in the counseling program. Moreover, several studies have reported fewer and less serious disciplinary reports among inmates in group counseling than among roughly comparable groups of non-counselees. Similar studies are being repeated with larger numbers of subjects who have had longer records of continuous attendance in group counseling. In future studies, more adequate controls will be used for better comparisons of those in the program and others who have not participated.

In the actual operation of group counseling the roles played by correctional officers in the program have contributed to the sensible recognition of the custodial necessities affecting the program. Because of their knowledge and understanding of security measures, correctional officers have helped their colleagues in group counseling to appreciate the viewpoints of custody and to avoid conflicts with custodial policies and procedures, as the group counseling program developed. By their contributions to staff discussions and by their advice in training sessions and on other occasions to group leaders not identified with or experienced in custodial functions, the purposes of institutional security and of treatment have been better and more harmoniously integrated in the group counseling program.

The question has been raised, "If material of custodial significance comes up in the group counseling session, should it be reported to the responsible custodial authority?" The question might be made more specific by the following examples. Suppose an inmate were to reveal an escape plot in the making or blurt out his role in a past stabbing incident, should the group leader report the statements to the custodial staff?

Actually, such instances have occurred so infrequently as to be insignificant in the experience of group leaders in the California prisons. If, however, something of the sort were to occur, the group leader is expected first to discuss the matter with his group. In a minimum custody facility, a man under obvious emotional strain openly mentioned his intention to escape in the presence of the group. The other inmates, after discussing the situation with him, made an unusual recommendation. They suggested that for his own protection the inmate contemplating escape be placed in the small "holding unit" of medium custody in the institution. With the consent of the group, the group leader promptly discussed this plan with the top custodial authorities in the institution and received their approval. The prospective escapee accepted the plan, and after a day or two in segregation regained control of himself. The man was subsequently paroled. There was no notation of his placement in segregation in his case file. In this instance, the group leader had been permitted to employ constructive treatment as a preventative rather than punishment, with the concurrence of the inmates in his group and the approval of the institutional administration.

When the group is not able to solve a problem caused by the revelation of some matter of custodial significance, then the group leader, with the

understanding and approval of the group, is expected
immediately after the session to consult with his
casework supervisor or with others in charge of the
group counseling program. What is done will then
probably be based on more adequate judgment and experience than if the group leader himself were
either to overlook the material or to proceed on
his own to divulge it to the correctional staff. The
group leader would feel more secure in sharing the
responsibility. The administrative aspects of the
matter would be more clearly defined and effectively
handled.

Promptness should be observed if any such
situation were to arise, but a guided promptness.
A solution should be sought that will avoid gossip
or excitement. What is decided should, if possible,
not give the inmates any basis for the belief that
their confidence has been betrayed. They are con-
sulted frankly by the group leader and their agreement is sought before any plan is put into operation.
If the group counseling program were ever to be regarded by the inmates as an administrative procedure
for getting "information", its discontinuance should
be considered. Indeed, it would probably be necessary. There are seven hundred counseling groups in
which there are ten thousand inmates in the program
in the California prisons. No occasions have been
reported when violation of the confidentiality of
group counseling has been necessary.

If, through taking advantage of the inmates'.
trustfulness, the group counseling program were to
get the reputation of being a source of custodial
information, if inmates who expressed strong feelings about institutional matters were punished, or
if the staff members who listened and did not report what occurred were reprimanded, group counseling would soon lose its effectiveness. The program
would be regarded not as a device for treatment, but
just another subtle indignity practiced by hypocriti-
cal authority upon both inmates and subordinate
staff members.

80

LIMITS TO DISCUSSION AND BEHAVIOR:

The question has been raised as to the procedure to be followed by group leaders when material
is discussed freely in the group which, if mentioned by inmates in other places in the institution,
might be a source of disciplinary action. An illustration may help to clarify this matter. An inmate
in a group session said that the warden's heart was
in the right place, but that in practice he was
actually only a salesman. Because the group sessions
represent a privileged situation, the remark drew
no critical reaction from the group leader. There
were a few smiles but the group did not follow it
up. That was the end of it, except that the leader
admonished the group that in counseling sessions
we tried not to discuss any personalities in the
institution other than our own.

In the group sessions, inmates may release
feelings of frustration or resentment or make critical statements without being "written up." Indeed,
an essential purpose of group counseling is the
airing or ventilation of attitudes and the release
of feelings. The specific items discussed are
secondary to this release of feelings, this emotional catharsis, in the presence of a permissive
person who does not reject or punish and in whom
the inmate has confidence and faith.

The maturity and security of the group leader
is the crucial factor. Group counseling is a treatment occasion. Critical comments made elsewhere in
the institution at other times by counselees in
the presence of the same group leader, would obviously be quite different in context and would
need to be considered administratively from a different point of view. The maturity of the group
leader and his experience may be taxed heavily in
the latter situation.

The behavior of inmates in the group may be

likened at times to that of children. When a child is thwarted by parental interference with something he wants to do, he may exclaim in anger, "I wish you were dead" in the presence of the mother or other adult. Or he may in milder terms just call the mother (and mothers usually seem to need to do most of the thwarting) "A mean old thing."

When the inmates call the staff names, this immature behavior is not very different from that of children or youth, who consciously or unconsciously, attribute their frustrations to the adults in their environment. A recent epithet about the staff, that impressed a group leader, was "leeches, living on the taxpayers." These reactions must be regarded not as insults or as violations of some rule or regulation. What is said must never be taken literally, but as the expression of attitudes toward authority or toward parents which are typical items in human psychology and which must be interpreted to be understood. Though such behavior is unpleasant, the worker will not need to react with personal resentment or hurt if he considers not the insulting words per se, but the feelings which underlie them. A possible parallel for the reader to think about would be the reaction of a surgeon to the odor of pus. He would not, if mature, be angry at his patient or think of punishing him because he himself felt personally affronted by the unpleasant smell from the wound. Such unpleasant experiences are to surgery what hostility is to penology. Both are expected and accepted concomitants of these occupations.

It must be understood, however, that there are limits to speech and behavior. Although there is much freedom of expression in group counseling, nevertheless one restriction or limit has been recognized as inviolable by the group. The counselor may permit hostility in speech, but not in overt behavior. If two inmates become so quarrelsome and antagonistic toward each other as to be on the

82

verge of fighting, it is the responsibility of the group leader to prevent any such aggressive behavior. It has not been difficult to avoid such episodes. Although at times strong feelings have been expressed, no actual instance of fighting has as yet been reported as having occurred during the many thousands of hours of group counseling in the prisons of California. This absence of overt behavior was also true during the earlier experience mentioned in Chapter 1, when group counseling was begun in 1944 and groups in the Reception-Guidance Centers were conducted by certificated teachers.

CUSTODIAL MANAGEMENT IN TRANSITION:

A great obstacle to the development of the treatment institution resides in the hearts of those sincere and conscientious administrators with deeply motivated feelings concerning custody. Their thoughts seem never to stray far from the needs for security measures. They do not realize sufficiently in their daily work that nearly all of the inmates sooner or later will again be free in the community. As parolees these men may sometime live in the same neighborhood in which reside close friends or even relatives of these employees. It is therefore to their own personal interest, as well as that of what is vaguely referred to as society, that men released from prison should have feelings about themselves and their relation to the people around them different from the resentments, the hostilities, and the self-justifications for their errant behavior which filled their minds and directed their lives when they came to prison. These conscientious employees must come to understand that the most important factors for the control of parolee behavior in society are to be found, not in the activities of police officers or parole agents, but in the hearts of the men themselves. If parolees are ever to be self-directedly on the side of authority, it would seem logical to believe that the feelings to support these attitudes will have to be established while they are still in the correctional institution.

Competent institutional administrators have long since become skeptical of such typical custodial strategies as the use of informers or stool pigeons. For one thing, the information divulged may be inaccurate or misleading. Again, an informer system usually involves custodial dangers, such as fights or even stabbings. But most significantly in relation to the present discussion, the atmosphere of the prison is poisoned by the presence and official acceptance of informers. And yet, one must also realize that many conscientious prison officials have confidence in the informer system and other similar devices and find security in their use.

Group counseling and other kinds of treatment through wholesome human relations, in contrast to the type of prison management characterized by the informer system and other similar devices, may make possible a more healthy psychological atmosphere in the prison. This may be recognized by the gradual growth among the inmates of responsibility for the wholesomeness of the institution. In group counseling, if the testing of the staff by offering information of a custodial character, such as telling about the proposed escape described above, does not result in betrayal by authority, then still more gradually and cautiously the inmates may come to accept a responsibility for protecting the institution against abuse, for example, by seriously disturbed inmates. On the positive side, the inmates may, as did a group of women at the prison in Corona, volunteer to work on week-ends and on holidays for a number of weeks to get out an unusually large order of clothing on time. They did so because of their respect and affection for the staff and especially the supervisors in the clothing factory. The shop was a situation in which the human relations were constructive influences. Shop foremen conducting

group counseling have reported unsolicited helpful suggestions from inmates to improve production.

The above examples represent violations of the
so-called "inmate code" which is more likely to
condone sabotage or the "slow down" than enthusiastic work. Perhaps these instances represent a
dividend from a treatment program which enlisted
the cooperation of the inmates and freed them to
express their kindly feelings toward others as well
as their hostile ones? May this also encourage the
hope that the outcomes of what is done to advance
wholesome human relations in an institution may
eventually become constructive substitutes for the
"informer system" and other unhealthy devices involving inmate-staff communication now used in
prison management?

THE RECONCILIATION OF INMATE AND STAFF VALUES:

Growth in inmate identification with the forces
of law and order within the institution is no simple
matter to accomplish. The points of view involved
strike at the depths of inmate and staff emotional-
ity. As mentioned earlier, because they are so
deeply engrained, some sociologists think the two
viewpoints are irreconcilable in the ordinary
prison. Likewise, many "experienced" prison employees hold the same pessimistic belief.

Each jail or prison worker has to study his
own attitudes. Some will arrive at a negative answer and perhaps strengthen their bias against the
possibility of enlisting genuine cooperation from
inmates to achieve a good climate in the institution. Others may temper their prejudicial concern
over security, and come to the realization that
though their primary job may be to make the institution as secure as possible, this purpose can be
reconciled with the belief that inmates who genuinely accept treatment may develop and evidence an
active desire to cooperate with the staff, even in
matters of custody.

Prisoners also may be skeptical regarding the possibility of genuine cooperation of staff and inmates. At San Quentin, during wartime, an inmate who had served overseas stated that one might get the cooperation of officers and men in a military unit, but that men in prison were different and not capable of such behavior. Shortly after this comment was made, the writer had occasion to call upon the loyalty of a group of inmates in a very difficult and for them a dangerous situation. Most of the men responded with outstanding courage and faithfulness. Unless prison administrators have the willingness to try more constructive methods of working with inmates, they may continue to preserve their skepticism regarding the possibility of achieving wholesome inmate-staff relationships.

Among prison inmates, the frankly insane, or the extremely hostile, aggressive, homicidal types would not be expected to accept the interest of the staff as genuine. In a discussion of the difficult problems in penology presented by the most extreme cases, the so called "mad-dog" prisoners, Justice Curtis Bok* has described them as incurable, unreformable and even unpunishable. What a tragedy for penology when the control of this small percentage of the prison population becomes a determining factor in the management of a prison! Vigilant precautions are necessary for inmates awaiting execution, for those with propensities to escape, those who are in prison for natural life,and for the small minority who are of a dangerously hostile disposition. The large majority of inmates may be best helped especially in the time preceding their release by transfer to institutions of lesser custody or to honor camps where they may practice self-directed behavior as training for similar desirable behavior after release to society

---

* See Bok, C., "Star Wormwood", New York, Knopf, 1959, 228 pp.

REWARDS FOR EMPLOYEES IN GROUP COUNSELING:

There are many compensations for those employees who participate in group counseling. One is the warm appreciation they receive from the inmates in their groups. The greetings received from his counselees, as the employee meets them in the course of his day's work, have a good and heartening quality. Over a decade ago, a magazine article* described prison work as the meanest job in the world. In happy contrast to this gloomy evaluation, employees in walled prisons have expressed with deep feelings the sentiment that since they have been engaged in group counseling as group leaders, their work has become much more pleasant and genuinely rewarding. Interesting, too are comments from some of them and their families that group counseling has carried over to their own homes and helped to improve morale there.

Men who have been employed in a severely custodial institution for many years have told the writer, sometimes with evident strong feelings as they did so, that they have had more satisfaction from their group counseling experience than from anything during the many years since they first joined the prison staff. Previously they reported having in their work a constant diet of tensions, fears, and boredom. By contrast, in the same prison after participation in group counseling, they reported experiencing greater opportunities for interest and enjoyment of their work.

Inmates or clients in correctional facilities or agencies will probably never like all that the staff members require of them. Neither do patients in a hospital enthuse over many of the necessary hospital routines. But it is not too far beyond expectation to hope that prisoners, parolees or

---

*   In the American Mercury for September, 1945.

probationers may some day, as treatment advances
in these agencies, accept the staff with appreciation,
as the doctors and nurses are accepted by patients
in a good hospital.

SERVICE AS A FOCUS IN WELFARE WORK:

What, if any, significance for workers in social agencies this account of the advancement of
reconciliation of custodial necessities and treatment objectives in correctional institutions may
have would depend naturally upon the circumstances
surrounding their agencies. If the attitudes of
ordinary citizens and those in positions of leadership in the government and the communities are
suspicious or otherwise severe and unfeeling toward
welfare recipients, then the less secure welfare
staff may be influenced toward introducing stringent
administrative methods consistent with the viewpoints of their employers, the general public. If,
on the other hand, the welfare recipients are accepted, with careful scrutiny of their cases, to
be sure, but also with sincere concern and the desire to do something for them as human beings with
problems, then the concepts of "service" or treatment grow in importance. Thus, the attitudes of
the leadership of the social agency toward service,
like those in charge of correctional institutions
toward treatment, naturally influence greatly how
the social workers are directed to approach their
clients.

In "The Road Ahead for California's Needy
Children", the viewpoint is stressed that service
be "a consistent focus" for the endeavors of workers
in the program. If this focus be accepted in the
welfare agency, then group counseling may be useful
because it may aid in the mutual acceptance of
clients and workers, as has been true of employees
and inmates in the prisons. If group counseling
and other kinds of service are successfully introduced, then not only may the clients profit

from these more constructive activities, but as was true of the employees in the prisons, the staff should feel a greater satisfaction and be more comfortable and happier in their work.

SUMMARY OF THE CHAPTER:

In this chapter, some custodial considerations in correctional work and administrative procedures in the welfare agency have been discussed. It is desirable to consider such matters thoughtfully, since members of the staff will raise them during discussions of the values and conduct of group counseling. It is reassuring to learn that custodial issues have not caused problems of serious consequence in the actual operation of the group counseling programs in the California prisons. In explorations of the use of group counseling in welfare agencies, the attitudes of the community and of the leadership of the agency toward welfare recipients are factors of significance. Both may be influential in affecting the attitudes and efforts of workers and the extent of their use of service as a focus in the treatment of their clients.

A primary purpose of group counseling is to further wholesome interpersonal relationships between inmates and employees in the adult correctional institution because such relationships are valuable and are a necessary prerequisite for a treatment program. If the good climate necessary for treatment is achieved, then the return of the inmates to society adequately prepared to adjust there would be accepted as the fundamental objective of the correctional institution in the minds of employees and inmates. Similarly the atmosphere of the welfare agency which has developed service as a focus will be a constructive influence not only for the growth toward maturity of the clients, but also for the morale of the staff.

CHAPTER 7

POSTSCRIPT

ACCEPTANCE OF SELF:

To believe in oneself as an acceptable person
is the very foundation of adjustment in society, for
only as a man feels himself to be worth liking can
he begin to feel more friendly toward others. If
group counseling is helpful in facilitating the better acceptance of self, then the client may also
develop better feelings about others and begin to
establish more satisfactory relationships with persons in authority, with fellow workers, with friends
and family. According to this hypothesis, good relationships with others grow out of good feelings
within oneself. As this growth in maturity occurs,
the hostility or indifference toward the world in
general, the expressions of exaggerated criticisms
of society observed in many offenders and among
clients of social agencies, may then begin to lessen.

Group counseling may be helpful because it offers the inmate or other client the opportunity in
the group sessions to put into words the destructive
feelings or other conflicts within himself. In the
presence of the leader and his peers in the group,
who may have problems not unlike his own, the counselee can express and examine his own destructive
or undesirable feelings about himself or others
without the fear or anxiety of incurring additional
rejection or punishment. Later he is protected,
moreover, from suffering in retrospect feelings of
embarrassment and self-reproach for having said
what he did, and thus increasing his feelings of
discomfort about himself.

In the adequately conducted group something

may happen psychologically within him, not easy to describe or to explain, which may be helpful in improving the client's feelings about himself. In the mysterious ways of the mind, this combination of acceptance by a parent figure, that is, by someone in an authority role, the group leader, plus the freedom of mind when releasing and examining disturbing feelings in his presence and before the group, as occurs in group counseling, has treatment values of great strength. When this has happened over weeks or months in the prison counseling groups, the counselees have reported that they have felt less troubled about themselves as persons and have been able to get along better with others in the institution, both employees and inmates. Observations by the staff and by other inmates have confirmed these improvements in their relationships with others.

GROWTH IN SELF-ESTEEM:

Something positive must be involved in the above mentioned changes in the attitudes of counselees toward themselves. Not only should the reduction of such feelings as discouragement or inferiority occur in the inmate or other client, but, more positively, the acquisition of feelings of self-approval or self-esteem need to be nurtured. The human interest and good will which characterize the leader's support of this growth in the client's personality through gains in self-knowledge, is a major dynamic factor in group counseling. Another is the recognition and encouragement which he gets from others in the group who are working toward similar advancement within themselves.

Efforts of the group and its leader to enhance the clients' self-esteem are important because in this area may be found a notable deficiency in the personalities of offenders and other clients. For example, the use of "Mister" before their last names in addressing inmates in the group helps to build their self-regard. This is in contrast to the

91

humiliating treatment of prisoners by the staff or by the inmates toward each other, when in a men's prison they are called "cons" or in a women's prison "girls." The reader may readily call to mind other sources of humiliation suffered by prisoners in jail or prison which are destructive of self-esteem. One might also ask, how might inconsiderate treatment which lowers self-esteem be experienced by clients in welfare agencies?

In the counseling group, individual contributions to the progress of the group should be recognized and the individual complimented by the group leader. This may be done in the form of a question to the group. The leader may ask, Do you think that Mr. A. has described how he feels toward persons in authority and the possible effects these feelings may have had in causing the behavior that got him into trouble?

As any counselee responds to treatment and growth is evidenced, in addition to the leader, the others in the counseling group need also to commend him. Experience has shown that under favorable auspices you may find recognition and applause for accomplishments in the counseling group, similar to what may be observed sometimes among a group of happy children at play, or in a classroom conducted by a sympathetic and understanding teacher. The forceful or dynamic impacts of these commendations in the group are tremendously important for the growth in self-esteem of its members. Thus, although group counseling is new as a technique in these and other ways, it utilizes resources deep in human nature itself, <u>the constructive influences of human beings upon each other.</u>

<u>THE EFFECTS OF AN ATMOSPHERE OF TREATMENT:</u>

According to our hypothesis, the experiencing of constructive feelings about themselves and toward others may be the foundation of greater self-direction and control in the inmate's way of life. The values of such positive experiences in the counseling groups are magnified in a supportive setting, like the psychological atmosphere found in an institution which is treatment-oriented. In the institutional environment, inmates may not only accomplish these desirable improvements in their feelings about themselves but also have them fortified to the degree essential to make possible their retention later when the individual returns to the community. In the treatment-institution, inmates may be helped to achieve and sustain the modest level of maturity necessary for passably good adjustment in society. The employees in such places will be persons who can accept the inmates as fellow human beings whose past errors are neither excused nor condoned, but who are in need of acceptance and encouragement to achieve greater maturity and by this growth in personality to abstain from future conflict with the law. For their part, the staff bring about a harmonious atmosphere by trying to appreciate each other's activities. In a community agency, wherein treatment is emphasized, similar but much less potent overall influences may occur.

In the general hospital, patients need to be restricted by regulations. For example, the hospitalized patient suffering from an acute infectious disease is isolated for purposes of hygiene and treatment. Again, hospital visiting is restricted to convenient hours. Diets are prescribed and enforced. There are many other necessary routines to be observed by the patients. In the treatment institution, likewise, disturbed inmates are removed from the general population. Regulations of hours of visiting and of eating, sleeping and other activities are necessary. These requirements are most sensibly carried out in the hospital or prison if the patient or inmate understands why they need to be enforced.

It is questionable whether inmate growth toward maturity can occur in a correctional insti-

tution unless limits are set and enforced as to
conduct in group counseling sessions or elsewhere
in the treatment institution or agency. In such
places, the staff accepts the inmates as persons
with troubles and in need of treatment rather than
punishment. All understand the values of such human-
ly sympathetic acceptance for the good of the client
and the best interests of society. But there is
never the absence of control, always defined limits
of inmate behavior are clearly-stated and enforced.
Effort is continuously made by the staff to make
sure that the client is fully aware of what he may
and may not do, in the group counseling sessions as
well as elsewhere in the treatment institution.

If the effects of these methods of instilling
an acceptance of control are lasting, the client may
continue, after the treatment is over, to derive
satisfaction from behaving in a socially approved
manner. Essentially, if group counseling is to attain these objectives, it must obviously be a growth
experience for the client, a growth toward more mature attitudes toward himself and others. He must
accept with understanding the circumstances of his
past life and have reasonably hopeful attitudes toward the present and the future. He must strive to
understand the importance of self-control in himself and others in a democratic society.

NEW ROLES FOR EMPLOYEES:

In the genuinely treatment-oriented institution,
no longer can one classify the staff as either custodial or treatment. Instead, the true correctional
employee is aware of both responsibilities. All on
the staff, especially those who are in personal
contact with the inmates, will in general display
an approximation of the desirable personality traits
listed on Chart I in Chapter 5. In their relationships with clients, employees will be genuinely helpful in their outlook. They will accept the treatment
role in their behavior on their jobs. But they will

94

also accept their responsibilities for the orderly operation of the institution or agency.

Inmates may not always obey the rules of the institution with joy and alacrity. College students, military recruits and many other persons likewise resent some of the regulations that they are required to obey. But persons of reasonable good will respect those who conscientiously and fairly enforce necessary regulations. Offenders in the treatment institution are encouraged to accept more willingly the necessary controls over their behavior.

Correctional treatment and social service are most effective when conducted in an institutional climate or an agency atmosphere which accords with these objectives. According to the primary hypothesis of this volume, the effectiveness of the treatment of offenders or of service to welfare recipients may be recognized as based fundamentally upon wholesome human relations. There is probably a more fundamental need in connection with treatment for wholesome human relationships to be present in the correctional institution or social agency than in the ordinary hospital. Thus, in the general hospital, if the surgery is good, in most cases the patient will get well. Only a stupid or insane nurse may interfere with recovery. In the prison, however, though the psychiatrist may be outstanding, if others in the prison do not support his treatment and are critical or sarcastic about it, the inmate may change very little or even become worse despite the good treatment in the prison's psychiatric clinic.

Correctional officers, shop foremen, teachers, chaplains, psychiatrists, psychologists and others work together in the treatment institution on a mutually understanding and appreciative basis. All accept the inmate as in need of training and counseling. All employees are guided by the positive function of helping inmates to gain better knowledge

95

of themselves and their problems and,they hope,to achieve thereby greater self-control.

In the treatment program, employees, whatever their rank or station, are self-respecting workers. Firsthand experience in group counseling, like that offered in the demonstration course for which this text has been prepared, and in the practical experience of conducting a group thereafter, may become part of the training and experience of all workers in the correctional agencies and institutions of the future. Not only treatment values, but also custodial security may be enhanced when this is done. An interesting example is an experience at the Tehachapi Branch of the California Institution for Men. Escapes were reduced considerably below earlier rates during the period after all inmates had agreed to participate in group counseling. Moreover, the entire staff, of whom one-third were actually conducting groups, all had recognized roles in accomplishing the treatment objectives of the institution.

TEAMWORK IN TREATMENT:

In closing we return again to Karl Menninger's concept of milieu therapy and the similar philosophy of institutional operation of Maxwell Jones in his description of the hospital as a therapeutic community. According to these theories of institutional management, no one group of workers, however specialized and authoritative, has all the answers to the many and diversified problems concerning the improvement of man's adjustment in community living. However, when all the employees in an institution work together as a genuine team, the resultant cooperative approach is considered by these and other eminent authorities in the social sciences to be much more effective for the welfare of all concerned.

Slowly but encouragingly in recent years one may note the transition of correctional and welfare

agencies toward places where the treatment of
clients is emphasized without any loss of consideration for the welfare of others in society.
Many obstacles, among which may be listed con-
servatism or other limitations in human nature itself, impede progress. Many problems of crime and
delinquency that could be better understood and
perhaps controlled, remain unsolved because of the
fear among leaders of trying new methods or devices and especially because of insufficient support of investigations of institutional and agency
methods of treatment and other lines of research
in the field of correctional and welfare work.

Progress is, to be sure, evident, but it could
be greater and faster -

> "Were half the power,
>   that fills the world with terror,
> Were half the wealth,
>   bestowed on camps and courts,
> Given to redeem
>   the human mind from error."*

---

* Quoted from "The Spanish Student" by
Henry W. Longfellow, Act II, Scene 5.

APPENDIX A

GLOSSARY OF TERMS.

This list of words has been selected because of their use in the text. The explanations are brief and designed only for the above purpose. Those who desire more comprehensive definitions are referred to standard psychological dictionaries or textbooks in psychology.

ADJUSTMENT - how one is able to get along with others and with oneself; thus, wholesome adjustment is the ability to meet reasonably well the needs of institutional or community living.

ADJUSTMENT CENTER - a place in prison where the most disturbed inmates are housed for treatment.

AGGRESSION - Examples of hostile aggression in speech are sarcasm or upbraiding; in action, bullying or attacking other persons.

ANTISOCIAL BEHAVIOR - activities which are opposed to the welfare of particular individuals or of society in general.

ANXIETY - a vague feeling of uneasiness or fear, or a tension a person feels without being fully aware of its cause.

AUTHORITARIAN - very demanding or domineering. The authoritarian person is seldom permissive and does not readily accept points of view, advice or suggestions of others.

CATHARSIS - the relieving of emotional discomfort by bringing its sources (fear, anger or other emotions) into consciousness and letting the client express these strong feelings.

CLASSIFICATION - a term used in penology to signify the program of individual diagnosis, guidance and treatment in prison. It employs clinical methods in the institutional assignments and segregation of inmates. This word may have different meanings in other fields of work.

CLINICAL - relating to expert advice or treatment by specialists. A clinic is an association of specialists.

CONTINUUM - A continuous series; thus treatment begins with superficial methods and becomes more complex gradually and without notable gaps, ending with the most technical and complicated methods.

CORRECTIONAL COUNSELOR - an important member of the staff of a prison with some training in the social sciences who compiles the personal and family histories of inmates, looks after the social problems of their dependents (wife and children), helps with their personal needs or troubles, veterans' rights, and the like.

COUNSELING - a) _directive_ - the giving of advice; the process or methods of discussing directly with the client his needs and problems for the purposes of helping him toward a good adjustment.

          b) non-directive - permitting and encouraging a client or a group of them to work out their own solutions of personal problems without the active intervention of the counselor.

COUNSELOR - a person who has had training in discussing personal problems with school children, college students, prison inmates or others. A friendly advisor; one who gives assurance, guidance or advice to persons with problems. When non-directive, the counselor encourages the client's own efforts to solve his problems.

CUSTODIAL CARE - the supervision of inmates designed to prevent escapes or disturbances within the prison and to make for smooth running of the institution. The modern prison also places emphasis upon treatment.

COVERT - covered, hidden, not clearly shown, as the feeling of a client who is friendly on the surface but actually is only pretending to be so.

DEEP THERAPY - treatment which reaches the heart of the emotional life of the patient or counselee - the unconscious disturbances which underlie deep-seated problems of personality.

DESIDERATUM - something needed and desired (Plural: desiderata.)

DIAGNOSIS - the use of tests or examinations (medical, educational, psychological, etc.) to study the personality and to ascertain an individual's needs in the way of treatment.

DISTURBED - over-active, noisy or destructive, showing strong emotion which is often more extreme than circumstances seem to justify.

DYNAMICS - see group dynamics.

EMOTION - deep feelings, such as love, fear or rage.

ESCAPISM - the tendency to run away from conditions that are unfavorable, or to retreat into day-dreaming and so get away from them in imagination.

FOLLOW-UP-STUDY - the use of field staff or other facilities to find out what has happend to institutional inmates after release.

FRUSTRATION - a state of mind which is distressing because normal outlets of thought or behavior are interfered with. Any interference with freedom of movement is frustrating.

GROUP COUNSELING - methods of orientation or guidance or treatment in which one leader may counsel a group of individuals or direct or facilitate constructive interpersonal relationships; a situation in which the interactions of the group themselves may have favorable effects upon those in attendance.

GROUP DYNAMICS - a term to indicate the influences of psychological forces in the group upon its individual members.

GROUP PSYCHOTHERAPY OR THERAPY - Psychotherapy is a method of treatment of problems of personality which is dependent usually upon verbal or other communication procedures, such as gestures, facial expressions, exclamations, bodily attitudes and the like. Sometimes drawing, finger painting, ceramics, toys, puppets, or other media are employed. Individual psychotherapy refers to situations where there is one therapist and one patient; group means more than one patient, sometimes more than one therapist may be present. Group therapy is conducted by psychiatrists, psychologists and social workers.

GUIDANCE - the process of utilizing the information obtained from the diagnostic study in giving advice to the client or the staff regarding possible lines of treatment, (work, study, religion or recreation) which may be helpful for the individual.

GUILT FEELINGS - anxiety over the transgression of prohibitions laid down by others or imposed by ones own standards and ideals. Guilt feelings also are related to the fear of punishment.

HOSTILITY - serious resentfulness, active hatred, which may lead to verbal or physical assaultive behavior.

HUMAN RELATIONS (OR RELATIONSHIPS) - how people influence each other; a panic is an extreme example of human relations in which people may cause each other to become terror stricken. It is contagious in character, like some diseases.

INFERIORITY - feeling oneself to be worse than others or unworthy, feeling ashamed of oneself. Inferiority feelings may be started by insults or other rejective behavior during childhood or youth when it is difficult for the immature person to handle the resulting distressing feelings.

INSECURITY - a troubled state of mind when the individual is uncertain about himself and his situation in life. The state of worry or fear accompanying present uncertainty and future dread.

INSIGHT - knowledge of the reasons for one's attitudes or feelings; as, for example, when the rivalry or hatred of a brother is recognized as a strong influence in causing similar attitudes toward colleagues in business or fellow workers in a shop.

INTROVERT - one who is turned in upon himself, that is, withdrawn, shy, thoughtful, as compared with the back-slapping, outspoken, active and talkative extrovert.

INTUITION - an indirect means of obtaining understanding. If this is of another person, it is in the form of a feeling or hunch about him based upon experience. It is not objective or clear-cut like a test score or an answer to a questionnaire.

MALADJUSTMENT - the state of not getting along well; an inmate who may be seriously out of line with institutional rules.

NARCOTIC ADDICTION DISEASE - the name of the sickness suffered by those habituated to taking drugs like heroin, which are habit forming.

NEEDS - wants or necessities. When needs are unmet, troubles may arise in a person's life.

NON-DIRECTIVE COUNSELING - a procedure or method of counseling in which the members of the group talk freely and without interruption and the counselor listens attentively and encourages this release of words and feelings without forcefully directing the individual interview or group counseling in any way. The counselor helps members of the group to arrive at their own explanations or answers to problems or personal disturbances and only rarely offers advice or information. The non-directive method is in contrast to the type of counseling in which the counselor answers questions and individuals or persons in groups spend most of the time listening and being directed toward thoughts and actions by the counselor.

OBJECTIVE ATTITUDE OR OBJECTIVITY - the ability to size up persons or beliefs without prejudice or bias. A fair and impartial way of forming a judgment. It is the opposite of subjective.

ORIENTATION - the means used to inform persons about some new situation in which they find themselves. For example, the newly received inmate is told about the circumstances of his life in prison.

PEER - one of the same rank, age group or social or occupational group. For an inmate, his peers are other inmates.

PAROLE AGENT - a member of the field parole staff, usually with training in social work, who looks after the social welfare problems of the parolee and his family. He helps them with personal needs or troubles, such as finding employment. He is also responsible for supervising the behavior and other aspects of the lives of parolees in society.

PENOLOGY - literally, the study of punishment. The word has grown to mean the study of correctional work in its broadest sense. The trained penologist of today is interested in treatment for rehabilitation, not merely punishment.

PROFESSION - a calling, occupation or vocation, engaged in for a livelihood which is understood and comprehended as to purposes and procedures by those employed. The correctional officer in a modern prison, if trained, is engaged in professional work because he understands the policies and methods of treatment employed with prison inmates and tries to act accordingly.

PSYCHIATRIST - a physician, a graduate of a medical school, with additional training in the care and treatment of mental diseases. To the psychiatrist are referred for diagnosis, for example, cases of persons who show strange or dangerous behavior.

PSYCHOLOGIST - professional student of human personality. A clinical psychologist is employed in the practical diagnosis and treatment of mentally aberrant and other persons, usually in association with a psychiatrist or other specialists.

PSYCHOLOGY - the study of human behavior or mental and emotional life; the investigation of human nature; the study of human relations, such as institutional morale.

PSYCHOPATH (or psychopathic personality) - a mentally unbalanced individual with little continuous self-control, usually not considered insane and yet likely to be a seriously maladjusted and troublesome person in an institution or community. More recently the term SOCIOPATH has also been used to indicate the socially maladjusted person who is not so mentally unbalanced as to require hospital treatment yet seems to be continually in trouble of some kind or other.

RAPPORT - good or positive feeling. Good rapport is evidenced by a comfortable and assured relationship between the counselor and the person counseled.

RATIONALIZATION - a term in psychology which means to explain something to oneself by arguments or reasons which are not really true. The sour grapes explanation is a good example.

REACTION - a response to something. It may be mild, like the blinking of the eyes exposed to a sudden light, or excited like the reactions of a crowd at a ball game when an unfavorable decision is given.

REALITY - the conditions in existing actual world.

RECIDIVIST - an offender who has been in custody on more than one occasion.

RECREATION - the improvement of well-being and happiness through games, dancing, physical exercises, reading, hobbies or other pleasant and enjoyable activities, including music, drawing, or other forms of artistic experience.

REHABILITATION PROGRAM - the means used to help clients understand their problems and gain the necessary self-control to manage their own affairs satisfactorily. It may include also various kinds of treatment to remedy defects and improve adjustment.

REJECTION - the feelings of rejection which occur in the state of mind of a person who believes he is unwanted or unloved, as in a child whose birth is resented by the parents; or the social discrimination of a rejected person in a minority group.

SECURITY - feelings of being wanted or belonging. A child has security when he knows deep within him that his parents love him.

SEGREGATION - placing different types of clients together, as younger men in a vocational type of reformatory.

SELF-CONTROL - the ability to control one's behavior, to avoid trouble by restraining or holding back impulses to speak or act in undesirable ways.

SELF-ESTEEM - one's own sense of personal worth, a person's feelings of regard for himself; good self-esteem is the opposite of inferiority or shame, yet it falls short of excessive pride or snobbery.

SHAME -worry or anxiety over the inability to live up to parental ideals, religious requirements or standards, or social standards. A person may be ashamed of his clothes if he feels they cause others to have a lower opinion of him.

SIBLING - Brother or sister.

SOCIAL STATUS - place in society. The social status of a family is the group or class to which it belongs, such as upper, middle, or lower class.

SUBJECTIVE - a form of judgment in which one's own desires, wishes, beliefs or feelings lead to the conclusions arrived at. Thus, a man who has been injured by a paroled prisoner might give the subjective judgment that all parole is a failure.

SUSPICIOUSNESS - distrust, a fear of being tricked or mishandled. Children who have been hurt by strangers become suspicious and afraid of them.

SYMPTOM - a sign of illness or maladjustment; thus, fever is a symptom of some diseases; alcoholism may be a symptom of deep worries or other troubles in the personality.

TENDER FEELINGS - those feelings which are kindly or socially desirable.

TREATMENT - actually all that is done in the institution or agency that affects the client. This treatment may be direct, as in education, or indirect, as when the family is cared for by the county welfare department.

VOCATIONAL TRAINING - a program of instruction under professional teachers, designed to prepare men for trades like carpentry, plastering, restaurant or janitorial work, autho mechanics or plumbing. Instruction may be "off-the-job" in a vocational classroom or "on-the-job" in a practical maintenance or construction project.

APPENDIX B

COLLATERAL READING

This text, "Group Counseling, A Preface to its Use in Correctional and Welfare Agencies", has been prepared primarily for workers in the Sheriff's Offices and in the County Probation and Welfare Departments. The purpose of the book is to explain the nature and objectives of group counseling and to indicate some potential values if introduced into these agencies.

An earlier publication, "An Introduction to Group Counseling in Correctional Service", was written primarily for employees in reformatories and prisons. Parts II and III of this earlier text are applicable to the starting of group counseling anywhere. They should be read especially by those contemplating an actual trial of the procedure.

A text for prison inmates was also prepared. It is entitled, "What Will Be Your Life?" This volume has been translated into Spanish. The use of this text for inmates has been optional in the prisons. Many group leaders have found it to be useful in stimulating discussion. Some have used it chapter by chapter in their groups.

There is considerable literature in group dynamics, including many theoretical and practical studies related to group psychotherapy. A few titles are given in Appendix C of the "Introduction to Group Counseling in Correctional Service". Readers may find some of these references of interest and value in their studies.

In the area of family counseling, the text, "Treatment in Prison, How the Family Can Help", may be of interest, especially to those in state correctional work. A revision of this text to make it more applicable to the families of those served by correctional agencies in the community, is now in preparation as part of the County Project. It should be ready for release early in the spring.

A third text, to be directed to the families of welfare recipients is also under consideration by the staff of the Department of Social Welfare of California. Their problems, different from those of the relatives of offenders, will be considered in the proposed volume.